The Power of

SELF-ESTEEM

The WorkSmart Series

The Power of SELF-ESTEEM

Samuel A. Cypert

amacom

AMERICAN MANAGEMENT ASSOCIATION
THE WORKSMART SERIES

New York • Atlanta • Boston • Chicago • Kansas City • San Francisco • Washington, D.C.
Brussels • Toronto • Mexico City • Tokyo

*This publication is designed to provide accurate and authoritative
information in regard to the subject matter covered. It is sold with the
understanding that the publisher is not engaged in rendering legal,
accounting, or other professional service. If legal advice or other expert
assistance is required, the services of a competent professional person
should be sought.*

Library of Congress Cataloging-in-Publication Data

Cypert, Samuel A.
    The power of self-esteem / Samuel A. Cypert.
        p.   cm. -- (WorkSmart series)
    Includes bibliographical references.
    ISBN 0-8144-7798-4 : $10.95
    1. Self-esteem. 2. Success--Psychological aspects. 3. Success in
business.   I. Title.   II. Series.
BF697.5.S46C97 1994
    158'.1--dc20   93-14310
                                                              CIP

Printing number

10   9   8   7   6   5   4

CONTENTS

PREFACE

I've spent the better part of a twenty-five year career in business trying to figure out why some people rise to great heights of success while others with the same, or better, qualifications—education, experience, and so on—drift aimlessly through life, never achieving anything particularly noteworthy.

In the course of those musings, I've written several books on related topics, and I have hired, trained, and attempted to motivate to high levels of achievement a sizable number of people. Sometimes it worked, sometimes it didn't.

The books afforded me the opportunity to meet many exceptional individuals, some of whom you, too, will meet in the pages of this book. I asked these achievers to identify the personal characteristics they developed and the practices they followed to achieve success. Most agreed that the principles are definite, specific, and transferable.

These successful folks also have another trait in common. They have a bias for action. They get things done. You'll find them wherever important people gather; they are usually in charge of the meeting. The action orientation of this book is the result of their influence on it.

Outstanding achievers are also very confident people. Because of their self-assurance, others may assume that such behavior comes naturally to them. Nothing could be further from the truth. We are all very fragile people, people who can be wounded by the slightest thoughtless word or deed, however unintentional, and we all develop confidence one success at a time.

When we encounter a setback, or when we are hurt by the insensitivity of others, most of us recognize the transitory nature of such feelings, and we quickly recover. We learn from the experience and usually become better people for having gone through it.

Unfortunately, for many, coping is not so simple. During the course of the research I've conducted over the years, I gradually began to realize that if one lacks the confidence to strive for success, knowledge of how to achieve it is meaningless. If our self-esteem is at such a low ebb that we doubt our ability to succeed, we'll never make the attempt. If we believe that we will fail, we most certainly will.

That realization led to this book. It is my personal conviction that we can all find comfort in the knowledge that almost everyone experiences moments of self-doubt. We can all learn from the lives of those who have experienced massive failures in their lifetimes, yet overcame them, and rose to positions of leadership in business, in politics, in the arts, and in virtually every other field.

When I made it a point to ask, others freely related their own experiences. Perhaps it was cathartic, or perhaps it was a desire to share their experiences so that others might benefit from them. Regardless of their motivation, I found their stories fascinating and their willingness to help uplifting.

Although I've been through the process several times, the amount of work required to produce one slender volume of prose continues to amaze me. In addition to the infrastructure of publishing professionals who contribute knowledge, skill, and ideas, there is also a corps of friends, associates, and family members who contribute ideas, critique manuscript drafts, and offer suggestions for improvement.

In the case of *The Power of Self-Esteem,* their advice was especially valuable. They were the guinea pigs whose willingness to take the self-tests and quizzes allowed me to improve and perfect them. I learned from these people and about them, and they learned about themselves as a result of the introspection demanded by the tests.

I am particularly grateful for the contribution of my writing partner and wife, Merrilee. Although my name appears on the cover of the book, many of the ideas contained in its pages are sharper and more universally applicable as a result of her contribution. In addition, her sustained support and encouragement during the writing process were invaluable.

Writing *The Power of Self-Esteem* also helped me to better understand myself. I was blessed with parents who, despite feelings of inadequacy that they no doubt experienced themselves, believed in me and taught me to believe in myself during my formative years. That early nurturing—so critical to the development of self-esteem—provided the foundation on which strong relationships with my own family and friends were built.

Knowing the doubts and fears that I have experienced—and continue to encounter—despite such stalwart underpinnings gave me a profound respect for the struggles experienced by those who may not have been so fortunate. For me, this book also helped place in clearer perspective the root causes of such frailties and provided everlasting hope in the knowledge that seldom do problems loom so large that they cannot be overcome.

I hope it will do the same for you.

S.A.C.

CHAPTER 1

"I AM SOMEBODY"

When Jesse Jackson speaks, this charismatic preacher, politician, talk show host, and founder and head of Operation PUSH (People United to Save Humanity), often exhorts crowds of followers to chant over and over these words: *I am somebody! I am somebody! I am somebody!*

That's the first step in acknowledging that each of us has the right to the respect of others simply because we *are*, because we exist. No other reason is required. We do not have to accept others' preferences and desires for ourselves. Every individual on earth should be entitled to choose for him- or herself what kind of person he or she wishes to be without explanation or justification to others.

There's a subtle psychological technique in Jackson's "I am somebody!" approach as well. The mind generally will come to accept what we tell it if we repeat the message often enough. It doesn't matter if what we say is true or not or if the statements are positive or negative; if we repeat the words often enough, we eventually believe them. Jackson's approach helps followers to counter negative feelings with positive statements. It's called self-talk or autosuggestion.

If you look at your image in the mirror every day for thirty days and repeat aloud fifty times—with conviction—"I am a good salesperson" or "I will get an A in this course," your mind will accept the statement as fact. Your confidence will improve, and you will be more willing to do the things (prospecting, polishing your sales presentation, making calls, or attending every class) that are necessary to succeed. Convincing yourself that you are capable is an important first step in reaching any goal.

1

CAUSES OF LOW SELF-ESTEEM

The experts say that very likely the most important element of developing self-esteem as children is for others to appreciate us for the unique personality traits, intellect, and aptitudes or talents that we each possess. No two of us are exactly alike, so we should learn early to measure our performance against our capabilities, not against that of our siblings or our peers.

If you had perfect parents as a child, you probably know all this already. If your parents, however, were mere mortals with the usual human frailties and foibles, the chances are good that you—like the rest of us—grew up to be slightly less than perfect yourself with the usual self-doubts and insecurities that plague us all. Occasional fears or feelings of inadequacy are a normal part of life, something to deal with and overcome.

Most feelings of low self-esteem stem from unhappy past experiences. When an important figure in our lives—a parent, a teacher, a boss, or another authority figure—made us feel inadequate, we began to doubt ourselves. The longer the criticism continued, the more we doubted until we began to believe that we couldn't do anything right. We accepted another's belief that we were inadequate regardless of the facts in the situation.

Some groups have had an even more difficult time. Women, as well as African-Americans and other minorities, still face negative stereotypes about their entire gender or race—despite the obvious fact that they as individuals had nothing to do with the distorted views of those who perpetuated their own cruel and unfair biases.

Women also carry the baggage of societal attitudes that link value and appearance. "Many of the most common day-to-day variations in the way women see themselves may be traced to how they feel about the way they look," says Sandra Haber, a New York City psychiatrist who specializes in the treatment of eating disorders, as reported in the

August 1991 issue of *Cosmopolitan*. "Appearance is associated with the whole person," she says. "What we see in the mirror is what we take into all our roles—lover, mother, professional. In fact we use self-image as a synonym for self-esteem."

All human beings tend to internalize failures, often giving them more attention than they merit. Because any failure looms spectacular in memory, we let it affect present and future actions far more than we should. Regardless of the scope of its magnificence, any defeat is temporary unless we allow it to be permanent. If we learn from the experience, we have taken a small step toward future success. It's a mistake we won't make again.

If you really examine the lives of successful people, you will discover that they have usually been characterized by some pretty spectacular failures. Abraham Lincoln failed as a storekeeper, a surveyor, a soldier, and a lawyer. Yet it was precisely those experiences that prepared him to lead the United States through its worst crisis—the Civil War. Lincoln became one of our greatest presidents in large part because of the empathy he felt for others as a result of his own difficulties.

Before Federal Express became a hugely successful airfreight company, founder Fred Smith experienced enormous setbacks. The company was on the verge of bankruptcy for years, Smith was personally prosecuted for fraud, and his own family sued him. Yet he persisted, and in 1990 Federal Express became the first service organization ever to win the coveted Malcolm Baldrige Award, the nation's highest honor for quality.

STARTING POINT TO IMPROVED SELF-ESTEEM

Regardless of your previous experiences, the good news is: It's never too late to learn and to change your opinion of yourself and your capabilities. The starting point of self-improvement is self-inspection. It begins with an honest assessment of your personal strengths and weakness and a burning desire to change the way you are.

It is important at the outset to realize that there are many aspects of our character and personality that contribute to our self-esteem. In an article in *Working Woman*, October 1991, Adele Scheele, a New York-based career strategist, management consultant, and lecturer, says: "One of the biggest fallacies is that there is such a thing as a fixed, 'true' self. After all, we behave differently in different circumstances.

"We are constantly adjusting our behavior to fit the situation. Think about it: We speak to our parents differently than we do to our children, or our staff, or our bosses . . . Who we are is a collection of selves—some more experienced and polished than others. If we view ourselves this way, there is more promise of change than if we cling to some absolute 'self' as if it were a Procrustean mold that we must torture ourselves to fit."

To change anything about yourself, you must also accept the fact that there are things you can control and things you cannot. Your low self-esteem is very likely the cumulative effect of the way your parents, friends, relatives, lovers, spouses, or any others who are important to you have treated you in the past. The key words are *in the past*.

You cannot change the past, but you can change the way it affects you. Put it behind you. Recognize that we can't control others or the way they treat us, but we can control our reaction to them. No one can make you angry or upset, no one can make you feel inferior or unimportant—without your permission and participation. It is simply impossible for another to influence any of your beliefs, feelings, or emotions unless you allow them to do so.

Make the commitment that you will no longer let others control your life or your reaction to them and the events they create. Take charge. Know that how you live your life is your choice and yours alone. Doing so does not require a radical change in your personality; it only requires a quiet commitment to yourself to put your past behind you, to forget about the times others have harmed you or treated you badly, to dwell on the possibilities of the future, not the failures of the past.

Use the following self-assessment test as a benchmark against which you will measure your future progress. Answer all questions as honestly and objectively as possible, as though you were evaluating a total stranger.

Self-Assessment
What's Gonna Happen If I Don't Change Anything?

I: Work and Careers

1. Do I really like the kind of work I do? _____
2. Will I be happy doing what I do for the rest of my life? _____
3. Would I do what I do regardless of how much I am paid? _____
4. Am I proud of what I do? _____
5. Do I often tell others about my job and career?

   _____
6. Did I make a conscious decision to go into this type of work or did it just sort of happen? _____
7. Would I be happier with a different job or career?

   _____
8. Am I driven to do what I do? _____
9. Am I usually enthusiastic about what I do, or do I have to sell myself on going to work? _____
10. How often do I work evenings and weekends?

    _____
11. Do I seek out challenging assignments or do I attempt to avoid them? _____
12. Do I look forward to Mondays or do I dread them?

    _____

13. Do I keep current in my field by reading and attending seminars on topics of interest? _____

14. Do I strive continuously to improve my skills and abilities? _____

15. How often do I think about changing jobs?

    _____

16. Do I like and respect my boss and my company's management, or would I rather work elsewhere?

    _____

17. Do I look forward to retirement? _____

18. What will I do when I retire? _____

19. When I retire, will I look back on my career with pride in my achievements, or will I regret not having accomplished what I should have? _____

    _____

20. If I won the $10 million lottery today, what would I do tomorrow? _____

II: Family and Relationships

1. Is having a regular lover or a spouse important to my self-esteem? _____ Why? _____

2. Is my self-esteem directly linked to the success of my relationship with my lover/spouse? _____

3. Is my sex life satisfactory? _____ If not, why not?

    _____

4. Does my spouse/lover meet my expectations?

    _____

5. Do I meet my spouse/lover's expectations?

    _____

6. Do I love my spouse/lover more than he/she loves me? _____

7. Do I often fantasize about others? _____

8. Am I often attracted to others besides my spouse/lover? _____

9. How often do I act upon my fantasies and attractions to others? _____

10. If I act upon them or if I do not, how do I feel

afterward? _____

_____

11. Is my relationship with my lover/spouse an equal partnership or do I do most of the giving and compromising? _____

12. How do I really feel about the old stereotypes of male/female responsibilities in the home? _____

_____

13. Do I insist on fair distribution of responsibilities outside of work or do I accept that I will always be expected to do more than others? _____

14. Am I liked and respected by my family and friends?

_____

15. Do I work harder at maintaining relationships (writing letters, making phone calls, socializing, etc.) than members of my family and my friends do? _____

16. Would I be saddened or relieved if I couldn't spend as much time as I presently do in maintaining relationships? _____

17. Am I often frustrated by the inattention and inconsideration of others? _____

18. Are others usually sensitive to my needs, or do I have to keep reminding them? _____

19. Does it seem that the only time others are considerate is when they want something from me? _____ Why? _____

20. Do I feel genuinely loved by those who are most important to me? _____

III: Rest and Recreation

1. Do allow time just for myself? _____ If not, why not? _____

_____

2. Do I plan for free time and how I plan to spend it, or do I simply take advantage of it as it occurs?

_____

3. Do I select free time activities, or do I usually participate in activities planned by others? _____

_____

4. How much of my free time do I spend in active pursuits such as exercise, sports, or strenuous play? _____

5. How much time do I spend in passive pleasures such as watching television, reading, or quiet hobbies? _____

6. How much time do I spend on spectator sports (watching football on TV or attending basketball games)? _____

7. Do I look forward to free time so I can accomplish something or so I can take a nap? _____

8. Am I satisfied with the mix of active and passive pursuits? _____

9. If I could do anything I wanted with my free time, I would _____

_____

10. How much of my free time do I spend on self-improvement such as attending night classes, seminars, self-study, or going to concerts, the symphony, or ballet? _____

11. Do I neglect other responsibilities (work, bill paying, chores) in order to have more free time?

_____

12. Do I prefer activities that I can do alone or do I prefer to be with friends or other family members?

_____

13. Do I take enough vacations? _____ If not, why not? _____

_____

14. Do I feel relaxed after a vacation, or am I disappointed and tired? _____

15. Do I plan vacations that I like, or do I usually try to accommodate the preferences of family, friends, etc.? _____

16. Are vacations really important to me? _____
17. Do I sleep enough? _____
18. Do I sleep too much? _____
19. Do I spend too much of my leisure time eating, drinking, or doing other things that are harmful to me? _____ Why? _____
    _____

20. What recreational activities did I pursue when I was young that I would like to resume? _____
    _____

There are no correct or incorrect answers to this self-test, nor is there a perfect score. It is intended to help you better understand yourself and to identify the things about yourself that you would like to change. Use it as a guide as you apply the techniques outlined in this book to improve your self-esteem.

THE POWER TO CHANGE

Just as a poor self-image is the result of failure (either real or perceived), healthy self-esteem comes from success. Seldom, however, does it come all at once. It comes from attention to the basics. Football games are far more often won by blocking and tackling than by the spectacular catches or dazzling runs that stick out in memory. Baseball games are generally won one pitch and one hit at a time. Home runs are the exception, not the rule. Seldom do we instantly go from aimlessly shuffling along to leaping tall buildings in a single bound. We repeatedly win small victories until one day we realize that we've won the war.

We often view self-esteem as a constant in ourselves, when, in fact, it is very fluid and differs for various aspects of our lives. When everything falls apart at once—work, love, sex, appearance, friendships, family—our sense of self-worth plummets. Every living person has ups and downs, times when we are on top of the world and days when life is the pits, but we feel insecure because we erroneously assume that we are the cause of all the problems. It's made worse because we somehow feel emotionally that we are the only person on earth who has experienced such failures even though we know intellectually that such an assumption is ridiculous.

Change is something we all inherently resist. Perhaps it is the fear of the unknown; after all, there is less risk in continuing to do things the way we've always done them. We sometimes refuse to change even when we know that not doing so will probably perpetuate the very problems we are trying to overcome. Until we reach the point that we perceive the pain of changing things to be less painful than the pain of leaving them the same, we are reluctant to do things differently.

In the 1992 presidential election, for example, all the opinion polls showed that voters were not so much "for" one candidate as they were "against" the others. Approximately 57 percent of the voters did not vote for President Clinton, but 43 percent concluded that the pain of maintaining the status quo was greater than the pain of change. That was enough to give Clinton the margin he needed to win the election.

Such knowledge in itself is helpful in dealing with change. When we feel the rush of self-doubt that often accompanies facing a difficult and important challenge for the first time, knowing that we are dealing with the fear of change helps us overcome it. Understanding that resistance to change is an innate human characteristic, one that everyone faces and must overcome, gives us the courage to try something new.

Answer the following questions yes or no. If the answers to more than half the questions are yes, you should begin to think about your options. If three-fourths are in the affirmative, the handwriting is on the wall in big red letters. If you answer more than 75 percent yes, the fat lady has already begun the aria. Make a change before someone else forces you to make it.

Are You Ready to Change?

1. Do you feel that you or others have set a hopelessly high standard for your performance? _____
2. Are you quickly bored with your work? _____
3. Do you long for new challenges? _____
4. Do you frequently worry about what your supervisors, coworkers, and subordinates think of you?
_____
5. Are you reluctant to take time off from work because you fear what will be waiting for you when you return? _____
6. Do you worry about the daily events at work when you should be relaxing and enjoying yourself?
_____
7. Do you have trouble finding something to talk about with people who are not connected to your work? _____
8. Do you take it as a personal failure when a project with which you have had minimal involvement fails? _____
9. Do you often feel that the fun has gone from your job? _____
10. Is work so sapping your strength that you have little energy for anything else? _____
11. Do you often find that those around you do not have the same level of commitment as you do?
_____
12. Are your coworkers less competent than you are?
_____
13. Are you frequently annoyed with them? _____
14. Are you often disappointed that others fail to recognize your contributions to your unit or company? _____
15. Do you find that you are less and less tolerant of the views of others? _____
16. Do you sometimes refuse to cooperate with others

even when you know it would be in your best
interest to do so? _____

17. Is it sometimes an effort just to be polite to those
with whom or for whom you work? _____

18. Do you get angry more quickly than you once did?
_____

19. Do you have fewer friends and socialize less with
people at work than you once did? _____

20. Do you often procrastinate on important jobs even
though you know you will pay the price later?
_____

21. Do you occasionally decide to ignore an order or
request because it is inappropriate or foolish?
_____

22. Do you ignore instructions at times because you
believe the person giving them doesn't have the guts
to enforce them? _____

23. Are you convinced that you could do your boss's
job better than he or she does? _____

24. Have you lost respect for your supervisor? _____

25. Do you envy your friends when they talk about
their successes in their jobs? _____

FLY ON YOUR OWN

There are specific actions you can take to begin building a
positive, healthy view of yourself, to take responsibility for
your life, and live it on your terms. Following are seven
techniques that you can apply to fly solo:

1. *Evaluate and accept.* Begin by critically reviewing your
strengths and weaknesses and deciding what you like about
yourself and what you do not. No one is perfect. Congratulate yourself for the things you like about yourself and vow
to change or ignore the things you do not, depending upon
their importance to your overall view of yourself.

2. *Examine your beliefs.* Do you have clear-cut values
and principles that you always live by? If not, you may be

too easily swayed by the opinions of others intent on using you for their own purposes. Make sure your foundation is strong.

3. *Take appropriate risks.* Life may be a crapshoot, but how often do you have to roll snake eyes before you begin to get the idea that the dice are loaded? Minimize risk by thinking the alternatives through carefully, but don't be afraid to try something new when the odds of success are in your favor.

4. *Learn from failure.* Mistakes are not permanent. Learn from them and move on to the next challenge. You will be a stronger person as a result of the experience, and next time you will be more likely to succeed.

5. *Live in the future.* Don't dwell in the past reliving failures or trying to revive previous successes. Look in the mirror and ask yourself: "What have you done for me lately? What do you plan to do for me tomorrow?"

6. *Choose positive influences.* Don't spend your time with people who belittle and depress you. If you are in a destructive relationship, get professional help. If you simply would like to improve your opinion of yourself, take a Dale Carnegie course, read a positive self-help book, or join a self-esteem support group.

7. *Demand respect.* If you do not like the way others treat you, tell them so. Let your friends, family, and coworkers know that you expect them to afford you the same courtesy and consideration that you give to them. Respect is seldom given freely. It must be earned. When others learn they can no longer push you around, they will stop trying.

We are all in the business of selling something—an idea, a dream, a budget, or ourselves. Several personal characteristics are listed below. Analyze your strengths and weaknesses as though you were a new product about to be introduced to the market. Be brutally honest. Fooling yourself now will only lead to trouble later.

Strengths and Weaknesses
Worksheet

Trait	Strength	Weakness
Good with people	_____	_____
Detail-oriented	_____	_____
Follow-through ability	_____	_____
Honesty	_____	_____
Appropriately packaged	_____	_____
Positive personality	_____	_____
Sound thinker	_____	_____
Decisiveness	_____	_____
Self-confidence	_____	_____
Accuracy	_____	_____
Sound job qualifications	_____	_____
Depth of current knowledge	_____	_____
Responsibility	_____	_____
Self-motivation	_____	_____
Attitude	_____	_____
Emotional control	_____	_____
Goal-oriented	_____	_____
Activity-oriented	_____	_____
Forward thinker	_____	_____
Integrity	_____	_____
Ability to deal with authority	_____	_____
Others:		
_____	_____	_____
_____	_____	_____
_____	_____	_____
Total	_____	_____

After completing this checklist, identify your three greatest strengths and your three most pronounced weaknesses. Develop a plan that includes specific details about how you can capitalize on your strong points and begin to overcome your weaknesses.

CHAPTER 2

ALL THE WAY WITH PMA

**They con-
quer who
believe
they can.**

—Virgil

Author, philanthropist, and multimillionaire W. Clement Stone has a positive mental attitude philosophy of success. At its foundation is a saying he often repeats: "What the mind can conceive and believe the mind can achieve with PMA!" The man who many regard as the father of the Positive Mental Attitude philosophy of success truly believes that nothing is impossible for the person who prepares for success, sets goals, and charges toward his or her objectives with enthusiasm and a positive attitude.

Stone defines a positive mental attitude as "the appropriate attitude under the circumstances." As he says in *Believe and Achieve* by Samuel A. Cypert, "It is composed of faith, optimism, hope, integrity, initiative, courage, generosity, tolerance, tact, kindness, and good sense. PMA allows you to achieve your goals, to accumulate wealth, to inspire others, to realize your dreams—however ambitious they may be—as long as you are willing to pay the price."

There is an important qualification in Stone's definition. The attitude that is "appropriate under the circumstances" is not the fanciful notion that if we simply look on the bright side—that the glass is half full instead of half empty—everything will work out. It won't, and the results will be even more depressing when it doesn't. A positive mental attitude is built upon the confidence that comes from studying, learning, thinking, taking action, making corrections, taking action again, and repeating the process until you succeed.

> **If at first you don't succeed, you are running about average.**
>
> —M. H. ANDERSON

OVERCOME NEGATIVISM

There's no such thing as a negative baby, believes Dr. Norman Vincent Peale, whose book *The Power of Positive Thinking* has sold tens of millions of copies in dozens of languages since it was first published more than four decades ago. "When we are born, the world is our oyster," he says in *Believe and Achieve*. "All we have to do is cry, and we get what we want."

We are taught to be negative, often by those who are most interested in our well-being—parents, teachers, law enforcement officials, and other authority figures who establish the rules for family life and society at large. As children, we are constantly told such things as "No, you may not touch the stove. It will burn you." Throughout our lives, we test the boundaries and are told again and again what we cannot do.

Such repetitive negative instructions have a cumulative effect. We begin to think more about the likelihood of failure than the possibility of success, and our thoughts become self-fulfilling prophesies. Because we think we will fail, we do. Whether we realize it or not, we regularly convert our thoughts into physical reality. Success in any endeavor begins with the belief that we will be successful; we then convert those positive thoughts into their physical counterpart.

The only way to overcome negativism is to stop negative thoughts when they occur and replace them with their positive equivalent. This is a difficult task to be sure when we've spent a lifetime developing the habits of behavior and thought that we practice. Seldom is it an easy process that can be accomplished quickly. In an interview in his apartment in Manhattan, Dr. Peale used a story to illustrate the point:

"We had a tree up at our farm in Dutchess County, New York, that was about two hundred years old and had begun to develop some problems. When we brought a tree man out to look at it, he discovered that it was rotten at the center and would have to be removed. Otherwise, a strong wind might come along and blow it over and damage the house.

"When the day came, the tree man and his helpers came out to the farm and I watched them as they began their work. I figured they would take out some gigantic saw and just saw the tree off close to the ground and that would be that.

"But they didn't do it that way at all. What they did was climb up to the top and snip off the little branches and work their way down until there was nothing left but the trunk. Then they took that down in sections until they had finally worked their way to the ground.

"That's the way you get rid of negative thinking. You start with the little negative thoughts and eliminate them and keep working on the bigger ones until you finally get to the center or core of your negative thinking. Then you eliminate it and you are ready to substitute thinking positively."

A LIFE OF ABUNDANCE

In his book, *You'll See It When You Believe It,* Dr. Wayne Dyer says, "It's possible to create happiness simply by focusing your thoughts on it . . . Quite simply we act upon our thoughts. Through them, we literally create our experience." He points out that we live in land of abundance in a society that places no limits or restraints on how happy or successful we can be.

"But there are some people—many perhaps—who dwell too much on what they *don't* have," Dyer says, as quoted in a July 1989 *Redbook* article. "This is what I call having a scarcity mentality. Such people have a constant refrain, which is, 'I would be a lot happier if I had . . .' These people believe their lives are lacking because they are unlucky, when in fact the problem is their belief system. As long as they believe in scarcity, that's what they will attract in their lives.

"The truth is that there are no limits to what is available to us in this endless universe. Once we truly know this, we will see this belief working for us in thousands of ways. Everyone I know who has moved from a life of scarcity into a life of abundance has learned to believe in this principle."

SOME WHO SUCCEEDED

The next time you're having trouble picking yourself up after you've stumbled, stop for a moment and count your blessings. Focus on the things you *have*, not the things you *don't*. Following is a list of people you have probably heard about and the things they overcame to achieve enduring success.

German composer **Ludwig van Beethoven** (1770–1827) became progressively hard of hearing. By his early thirties, hearing was difficult for him; by age 46, he was completely deaf. Yet, he wrote his greatest music during his later years.

French actress **Sarah Bernhardt**—the Divine Sarah (1844–1923)—was regarded by many as one of the world's greatest stars of the stage. She had her leg amputated as a result of an injury in 1914, but she continued to act until just prior to her death.

Louis Braille (1809–1852) was blinded at age 3. He became a teacher in Paris and developed the Braille system for the blind.

Novelist **Miguel de Cervantes** (1547–1616) lost his arm in battle and lived in poverty most of his life. *Don Quixote* and his other works have made him perhaps Spain's most prominent literary figure.

Helen Keller (1880–1968) was blind and deaf by age 2, yet she became one of America's best-known and well-loved figures. A hugely successful lecturer and author, she wrote ten books and many other works.

U.S. president **Franklin D. Roosevelt** (1882–1945) taught Americans that "we have nothing to fear but fear itself" during the height of the Great Depression. He was paralyzed by polio at age 39, but went on to become one of America's most beloved and influential leaders, elected to the presidency four times.

Henri de Toulouse-Lautrec (1864–1901) was deformed, crippled, and stunted. An inspired artist, his renderings of performers at Paris's Moulin Rouge cabaret elevated him to the pinnacle of the art world and gave him lasting fame.

Dr. Henry Viscardi, Jr. (1912–   ) was born without legs but served as a Red Cross Field officer during World War II. He is the president of the Human Resources Center, founder of Abilities, Inc., has thirteen honorary degrees, and has written nine books. He has served as an adviser to several presidents on issues related to the handicapped.

MAKE THE COMMITMENT

One of the greatest gifts of life is that we cannot foresee the future. The prospect may be alluring at times, but imagine the sheer boredom, or terror, that would accompany an existence in which we knew in advance all the things—good and bad—that would happen to us. There would be no surprises, no celebrations of success, no tears of sadness, and very little to motivate us. Why would we work harder to overcome obstacles if we already knew the outcome?

The most difficult part of any job is getting started.

—ANONYMOUS

Life is in many respects similar to taking a long trip in an automobile. We know where we are and we know where we would like to go, but there are two ways to go about getting there. The first is to hop in the car and go, working out the arrangements along the way. The second is to plan in advance, mapping out the route, determining the distance that we plan to cover each day, and so on. Either method will probably get us there, and although the first approach may be more adventurous, the second is likely to get us there far more quickly with much less stress.

We see the obvious benefit in planning a trip, yet when it comes to things far more important—our lives and careers—we often assume that events will somehow take care of themselves. We expect to make a lot of money, raise a perfect family, and be happy and fulfilled without having a definite plan of how to go about it.

The first step toward a happy and successful life begins with a commitment to create one for ourselves, to focus on the possibilities, not on the shortcomings. Doing so means focusing on the future, not dwelling on the past. We may not be able to foretell the future, but we can create it. Our reality will be what we make it. If we approach it positively and enthusiastically, we will attract positive results. Unfortunately, the reverse is also true. Unlike in a magnet, negatives do not attract positives. Negativism attracts failure and despair.

THE COURAGE TO CHANGE

Changing anything about yourself requires a great deal of courage, determination, and enough persistence to stay with the job until it's done. Transforming yourself from a negative or neutral person into a positive thinker is especially difficult because it goes against the tide of conformity. Positive thinkers are in the minority in every group. At work, at school, at social events, or at home, the general trend in thought and word is to focus on reasons why something won't work rather than why it will.

Negative thinkers may mask their views with such disclaimers as "let me play devil's advocate for a moment," or "just for the sake of argument," but the result is the same. They try to find reasons not to adopt a new idea rather than to concentrate on its potential. Any new idea involves risk, sometimes a great deal of it, but nothing worthwhile was ever achieved without the willingness to try something new.

Have the courage to be different without being contrary—without flaunting your independence. The quality that makes us interesting, that makes us outstanding personalities is the courage to be ourselves.

—ANONYMOUS

BUILD CONFIDENCE

There is something magical about self-confidence. Men and women who exhibit it attract more than their share of attention from others and they advance further and faster in their careers. They somehow seem to have been born under a different star. Success comes to them easily and naturally.

If you dig a little deeper, however, you will probably find that their confidence is the result of a long painstaking process that any one of us can employ. For some, it comes easier and more naturally than for others, but the process is the same. The principles are easily learned and can be applied by anyone. Following are some techniques that you may employ to become a positive thinker, a confident person who sees success possibilities instead of the potential for failure:

• *Associate with positive people.* Your mother was right when she told you that you would never bring the friends she disapproved of up to your level. They will only drag you down to theirs. It is much more difficult to be positive when you associate with negative thinkers than it is when you spend your time with those who have learned they can achieve their goals if they believe they can.

• *Make a list.* One of America's wisest leaders, Benjamin Franklin, is said to have made critical decisions by dividing a sheet of paper into two columns labeled pro and con. He then listed all the reasons for and against a particular course of action. The technique not only helped clarify his thinking, it graphically illustrated which approach had the most support.

• *Learn from experience.* If you have a tendency to be negative, review your behavior each day while it is still fresh in your memory. Analyze your actions and determine what you should do differently to become more positive.

• *Set aside time for thinking.* Make sure you allow at least a half-hour every day for thinking and planning. Go to a quiet place where others won't bother you. Relax. Think about your goals, measure your progress to date, and decide what actions you must and will take to achieve them.

• *Force yourself to focus on the positive.* When negative thoughts creep into your thinking, stop and reconsider. Make it a habit to look for the reasons why you *can* do something instead of those why you *can't*.

• *Learn to empathize.* Look at the situation from others' points-of-view. Try to understand why they behave as they do and what you can do to have a more positive, constructive relationship with them.

• *Initiate conversations.* Most people are shy. If you are reluctant to talk to strangers or casual acquaintances, you are in good company. Surveys show that 40 percent of adults consider themselves to be shy. *Assume* that the other person may be shy and take the first step to begin a conversation.

• *Bestow compliments generously.* A sincere compliment will go a long way toward establishing positive relationships with others and make you feel good in the process. Even if you don't like the person, congratulate him or her on an achievement. You may find that you've misjudged each other.

• *Avoid stressful situations.* If petty arguments upset your day before you leave home, try leaving before other family members begin the usual morning rush. Go to work early occasionally, catch up on chores you've been avoiding, or read the newspaper with your morning coffee.

• *Begin the day positively.* Think about the things for which you are grateful, the things that make you happy, not the problems, and all the things you wish you could accomplish but probably never will.

• *Take a break.* When you find yourself becoming annoyed by others or situations you cannot control, get away from them for a few minutes. Do something entirely different for a while. You'll be able to approach the problem more objectively after you've cleared your head.

• *Be realistic.* Set achievable goals for yourself and break them into bite-size pieces. Try to do at least one thing every day that moves you toward your goal. Small daily successes give you the confidence to attack larger, longer term objectives.

• *Take calculated risks.* If you never take a chance, you will never achieve anything worthwhile. Risk rejection of your idea as long as you're convinced it is sound. Attempt to meet new people and make new friends. Some won't respond, but others will.

• *Learn new things.* In today's fast-paced, high-tech world, if you are not learning, you're dying. Most of the knowledge a new college graduate has today will be obsolete in a few years. It's even more important to keep up if you've been out of school longer. Learning is not only interesting, it makes you more interesting to others.

• *View setbacks constructively.* As with a weight lifter, it is the resistance that makes us strong. We start small and regularly increase the resistance until we can lift more than we ever dreamed possible at the beginning. A failure is a learning experience. Nothing more.

• *Think before you speak.* If you have a habit of talking first and regretting it later, learn to hold your temper. Work on it a little each day until you have it under control. When you say something you regret, it's your positive attitude that suffers most.

• *Dress appropriately.* Look around you. If the people you work with wear suits instead of dresses or pinstripes instead of blazers, do the same. Nothing ensures confidence like the knowledge that you look good and others know it. It also keeps them focused on your capabilities instead of wondering why you look different.

• *Take care of your health.* Exercise regularly and stay in shape. It is much harder to maintain a positive attitude about yourself when you feel lazy, overweight, or lethargic. A little exercise goes a long way toward improving your self-confidence.

• *Help others.* Do something nice for someone without expecting anything in return. It keeps them off balance and it makes you feel great about yourself.

POSITIVE POTENTIAL

It has often been said that the human brain is much like a supercomputer, one that is far more efficient and powerful than even the most advanced manufactured device. The brain is similar to its mechanical counterpart in many ways, but particularly in this respect: We get from each what we put into it. It's the garbage in, garbage out (GIGO) theory of computer programming.

If we allow our human computer to be controlled by the negative influences all around us, the majority of our impulses will be negative. We will be controlled by negative thoughts, fear of failure, and the reluctance to risk anything new. However, if we eliminate negative thoughts, much as Dr. Peale's landscapers snipped away the branches of a decayed tree, we can begin the process of replacing negative thoughts with their positive equivalent.

In the forest it is impossible for most young saplings to flourish until older, larger trees have been removed. Sunlight cannot penetrate the leafy branches of mature trees to reach the forest floor and provide nourishment essential for life and growth of new seedlings. When a mature tree is removed, a miraculous thing occurs. In the space of a few weeks, the ground is covered with new growth. Seedlings sprout up everywhere, each reaching for the sun that was previously unavailable to them.

So it is with negative attitudes. When we have removed all the little negative thoughts until we have reached the core of our negativism, we are prepared for new positive growth. If we nurture and protect positive thoughts from the hostile environment that seeks to destroy them, they will gain the height and stature necessary to survive in a negative world.

Every living person has the potential to be positive, negative, or neutral, but potential is meaningless without action. Until we begin to do the things that are necessary to transform the way we think, we can never realize the great benefits of life that are ours for the taking.

CHAPTER 3

GREAT EXPECTATIONS

The problem most of us face once we make up our minds that we are going to change our lives for the better is that we expect to go from stumbling aimlessly along to leaping tall buildings in a single bound. When we fail, we become discouraged and give up, rationalizing that it was a bad idea anyway, or that it was something simply beyond our capabilities. Failure makes us feel even worse about ourselves and our abilities.

Making the decision to change is the easy part. Getting the job done is a lengthy, lonely, tedious process that requires a commitment that will sustain us no matter how tough things get or how much we're tempted. The habits we're trying to change have been developed gradually over a long period of time, and they will be eliminated the same way. In fact, we don't recognize our habits as such until they are so firmly ingrained that they are extremely difficult to break.

Self-help groups recognize how difficult it is to make a major change in your lifestyle, and they use a variety of techniques—peer pressure, reinforcement, group discussion—to aid the process. Nevertheless, in the end it is always an individual matter. We must break habits the same way we formed them: one drink, one cigarette, or one Twinkie at a time.

To think that we must immediately stop drinking, smoking, overeating, or indulging in any unhealthy or destructive habit is overwhelming at first. Instead, we vow that we won't drink the *next* cocktail, smoke the *next* cigarette, or eat the *next* candy bar. We know we can avoid one destructive behavior; beyond that we're not sure. Eventually, though

The chains of habit are generally too small to be felt until they are too strong to be broken.

—SAMUEL JOHNSON

we're never completely cured of the desire, we see ourselves as recovering from a drinking, smoking, or overeating problem. Gradually, our self-image changes and we no longer see ourselves as addicted to alcohol, cigarettes, or food.

We've also learned that it helps to replace a negative habit with a positive one. Dieters and those trying to quit smoking find they achieve better results when they introduce an exercise program into their daily routine. Instead of hanging out in bars with former drinking companions, alcoholics join Alcoholics Anonymous and form new friendships and alliances aimed at helping them change their behavior.

To successfully change any behavior, we must first eliminate the undesirable behavior and replace it with a more constructive one. Psychologist B. F. Skinner found that rewarding pigeons with food when they pecked a certain key taught them to behave in a certain way. They learned to peck that particular key whenever they were hungry. As quoted in Berkman's and Gilson's *Consumer Behavior*, Skinner called behavior modified by the consequences of that behavior "operant conditioning."

Of course, human beings are far more complex than animals or birds. We have a wide range of feelings and emotions, and more important, we can think. We do not instinctively respond to a stumulus as animals and birds do. Or do we? In the most basic sense, responding to stimuli is how habits are formed. We try something, we like it, and we keep doing it until it becomes a habit.

THE SELF-ESTEEM HABIT

Mental habits are formed in the same way their physical counterparts are. Our opinions of ourselves are based on a range of experiences, both positive and negative, that we have accumulated over the years. When we try something that doesn't work out as planned, we tend to internalize the experience. If others discredit an idea the first time we present it, for example, we will feel far less secure the next time around. If we keep failing, rather than realistically examining the idea itself for flaws, we assume that we are incapable of developing a workable idea. Eventually we stop trying.

The ability to evaluate our ideas and actions objectively and modify our behavior accordingly is critical to maintaining self-esteem. When others question our idea, the natural reaction is to defend it. If we become too defensive, we may alienate others who might be important to us in the implementation of the idea, and we may miss out on a modification that would make a pretty good idea a great one. A constructive criticism is not necessarily a personal attack. Accept it as such and put it to good use.

Of course, there are certain personality types who delight in discrediting others and minimizing the contribution of anyone besides themselves. Such negative, destructive people are generally recognized for what they are and discounted by those who really matter. Respond to them if you must, ignore them when you can, and never, never let them get to you.

EXPECTATION MANAGEMENT

Most professional services consultants—accountants, lawyers, management consultants, and such—understand very well the importance of managing the clients' expectations to ensure the success of the entire project. If the client is expecting one thing and they deliver another, the job is a failure regardless of its inherent quality and the thoroughness with which the assignment was conducted.

To avoid such misunderstandings (and subsequent problems collecting fees), the professionals spell out very carefully at the beginning of the project what they will deliver and what they will not. The scope of the engagement, interim, and final deadlines, the review process, fees, and the final "deliverable" (finished report, action plan, next steps, and such) are clearly explained in the agreement.

There's a good lesson for all of us in this approach. We are all finite people with specific abilities, knowledge, experience, emotions, feelings, values, and expectations for ourselves and others. When we are unrealistic in our expectations for our performance, we set ourselves up for failure, and the consequences can be even more destructive to our self-esteem.

Following is a short quiz aimed at helping you determine if you are realistic in your expectations for yourself. Circle the letter indicating the answer that fits you best. Answer each question or statement honestly; answers are at the end of the quiz.

ARE YOU TRYING TOO HARD OR NOT HARD ENOUGH?

1. How often do you measure up to your expectations for yourself?
   a. Occasionally
   b. Frequently
   c. Always
   d. Never

2. How large of a role did your position in the family (only child, firstborn, middle child, youngest) play in the development of your expectations for yourself?
   a. No influence
   b. Modest influence
   c. Major influence

3. What is your reaction to the statement, "Being in the right place at the right time is the single most important determinant of success"?
   a. Agree
   b. Strongly agree
   c. Disagree
   d. Strongly disagree

4. What is your reaction to the statement, "Persistence overcomes all obstacles"?
   a. Agree
   b. Strongly agree
   c. Disagree
   d. Strongly disagree

5. In most situations or problems, there is (are) usually:
   a. One right answer or approach
   b. Several solutions, any one of which may be acceptable
   c. No right or wrong answer, only perceptions of correct or incorrect answers

6. What are you most likely to do when faced with a major decision or problem?
   a. Put off making a decision as long as possible
   b. Hope the problem will work itself out
   c. Take the appropriate action quickly
   d. Take inappropriate action quickly

7. When your boss congratulates you on a job well done, how do you feel?
   a. That you deserve the recognition
   b. That you were lucky this time
   c. Grateful at first, doubtful later

8. How do you prefer to work?
   a. Alone
   b. With a team
   c. Alone, but periodically check your work with others

9. How often do you ask for help from others at work, at home, or in your personal life?
   a. Occasionally
   b. Frequently
   c. Almost never
   d. Never

(continues)

10. How do you most often feel about your life in general?

   a. I have total control of my life. It will be what I make it.

   b. I have some control of my life, but it is often influenced by factors out of my control.

   c. My life is almost always controlled by people or events that I cannot control.

How to Evaluate Your Score

1. If you chose **b**, you are pretty realistic about your capabilities. If you always meet your expectations, you are probably not stretching. If you measure up only occasionally—or never—you are being too hard on yourself.

2. The most desirable response is **b**. We are all influenced to a degree (perfect firstborn or only child, rebellious middle child, easygoing youngest, and so on), but the influence is usually modest. Acknowledge the family influence and adjust your attitude to compensate for any negatives.

3. Either **a** or **c** indicates that you are more pragmatic about accepting responsibility for your own life. A stronger response to the statement indicates you may be placing undue emphasis on fate. **b** warns that you may not be trying hard enough, whereas **d** hints that you may unrealistically believe you can overcome any obstacle.

4. Again, **a** or **c** is preferred. If you chose **b**, you are likely to be a perfectionist; if you chose **d**, you are a stoic. Either extreme indicates that you are probably being unrealistic in your expectations for yourself.

5. The preferred choice in our imprecise world is **b**. If you chose **a**, you tend toward perfectionism; **c** would indicate that you believe you have

little or no control of the outcome and no responsibility for your fate.

6. If you chose **c**, you are a decisive, action-oriented person. Answers **a** and **b** are warning signs that you may procrastinate to avoid having to make hard choices; **d** indicates that you expect too much of yourself.

7. An **a** answer shows that you have a healthy attitude toward your achievements. If you chose **b**, you are probably capable of more; a **c** answer indicates that you tend toward being an overachiever.

8. If you chose **c**, you are a confident person who can work with others, but you are quite capable of performing alone. An **a** answer cautions that you're trying too hard; **b** indicates that you are reluctant to accept responsibility and may not be trying hard enough.

9. Everybody needs somebody sometime, as the song goes. The key is not to overdo it; **a** is the preferred response. If you chose **b**, you may be too dependent on others. Answers **c** and **d** show that you tend toward perfectionism.

10. The more realistic choice is **b**. An overachiever might erroneously assume that nothing is impossible and choose **a**, whereas an underachiever would lean toward **c**.

The purpose of the quiz is to help you determine if your expectations of yourself are reasonable. If you always aim too high, you will be disappointed when you fail; if you expect too little from yourself, your self-esteem will suffer because you know that you could have done better. A healthy self-image is one in which you recognize your strengths and weaknesses and build on your strong points and work on your weaker ones.

It is also important to stretch occasionally. If your expectations are realistic most of the time and you regularly achieve what you set out to do, aim a little higher now and then. If a particular challenge appeals to you and careful analysis indicates that you have a good chance of success, accept the challenge. It will give you the opportunity to grow and the experience itself will make you stronger.

> It's hard being perfect in an imperfect world.
>
> —ANONYMOUS

YOU'RE OK, THEY'RE OK— BUT I HAVE TO BE PERFECT

If your answers to the preceding quiz show that you have a tendency toward perfectionism, perhaps a special word of caution is in order. Perfection is a warning signal that you have unrealistically high expectations for yourself and for others. You are also well on the way to making yourself miserable for life, since perfection is almost never attainable. Striving for excellence is an admirable quality; striving for perfection is a futile quest.

Analyze your motives. Why do you feel compelled to be perfect in everything you do? Are your motives internally driven or are they a response to others' expectations? If you are attempting to be perfect because someone else expects you to be, it's time to take charge of your own life. If your drive for perfection is internal, it may be a mask for insecurity. Because you feel inadequate, you overcompensate.

Build your self-confidence by setting realistic goals for yourself. Choose one or two things that are most important to you and focus on them. Adjust your priorities to allow the time necessary to do the job well. Learn the difference between excellence and perfection and don't be too critical of your performance when it falls short of perfect.

Play the "what if?" game. Imagine the worst case scenario and decide if you can live with the consequences. Let's assume you are late for an important appointment. Stress begins to build and you soon lose all sense of perspective.

Ask yourself: What's going to happen if I am late? My client will be upset. I probably won't get the order. If I don't get the order, I won't make my sales goal. If I don't make my sales goal, I'll lose my job. Logic would dictate, then, that if you are late for an appointment, you'll be fired.

Of course, that's ridiculous. If you are late for an appointment, you can probably explain the situation and your client will understand. Such things happen to everyone occasionally. Even if this particular client is totally unreasonable and you do lose the order, even that is not the end of the world. There are other clients and prospective clients, and you will have plenty of other opportunities to reach your sales goal. Learn to separate reasonable concerns from unreasonable fears.

THE DIFFICULTY WITH CHANGE

What would you attempt to do if you knew you could not fail?

—DR. ROBERT SCHULER

The principal difference between human beings and other animal species is that we alone have the capacity to decide what we will be. We are not ruled by instinct. Our ability to think and reason allows us to choose for ourselves what we wish to accomplish in life and the kind of person we wish to become. No other creature has that choice.

All too often, however, when faced with such decisions, we ignore them in the hope that things will work out for the best if we leave them alone, or we give up too soon when the desired change doesn't occur quickly or easily enough. Use the following worksheet to analyze your motives for changing yourself and why it sometimes does not work as planned.

Why Doesn't It Work When I Try to Change?

1. What exactly am I trying to change about myself? (Be as specific as possible. For example, "I want to overcome my habit of procrastinating.") _____

_____

_____

2. Have I truly been realistic in my expectations for changing my habits or have I tried to do too much at once? _____

_____

_____

_____

3. Do I generally accept change easily or is it always difficult for me to do things differently from the way I've always done them? _____

_____

_____

_____

4. Do I genuinely want to change for myself or am I responding to another person or a specific situation? _____

_____

_____

_____

5. Do I usually go public with my plans to change something about myself and feel embarrassed when I fail, or do I keep my plans secret so no one else will know if I don't achieve my goal? _____

_____

_____

_____

_____

6. Do I form new friendships and relationships easily or are they difficult for me? _____

_____

_____

_____

7. Do I have trouble with change in my career (accepting difficult new assignments or changing jobs, for example)? _____

_____

_____

_____

8. Do others consider me a flexible person? _____ Why? _____

_____

_____

9. Do I consider myself to be a flexible person? _____ Why? _____

_____

_____

10. Do I accept new challenges enthusiastically or fearfully? _____ Why? _____

_____

_____

_____

This worksheet helps you assess your willingness to change. Use it as a guide to understanding yourself and why you may not have been as successful as you would have liked in previous attempts to change. Be sure to consider your "change resistance quotient" when you develop your goals and plans in subsequent chapters.

Making a major change in yourself is a difficult and time-consuming task, one that is never easy. Someone once observed that it is similar to eating an elephant. It can be done, but only if taken in small bites over a very long period of time.

REALISTIC EXPECTATIONS

Look well into thy-self; there is a source of strength which will always spring up if thou wilt always look there.

—MARCUS AURELIUS

A happy, productive, fulfilled life comes from only one source: ourselves. The external environment can influence and affect our attitudes and emotions, to be sure, but in the final analysis, how we react to outside influences is our choice and ours alone. Since every individual is different in tastes, wants, desires, and needs, it may well be that happiness, like beauty, is in the eye of the beholder. We all crave different things, and as we grow and mature, we change and so do the things that bring us pleasure.

One thing is certain for each of us, however. Happiness is more than the mere absence of unhappiness. As reported by Kathy Ullyott in *Chatelaine*, December 1990, Dr. Michael Fordyce, a psychology professor at Edison Community College in Fort Myers, Florida, found that most of us experience momentary happy moods, "but a truly happy individual manages to lead (his or) her life with a sense of emotional well-being and contentment, an overall feeling of satisfaction."

Fordyce also points out that simply avoiding things that make you unhappy does not make you happy; it only makes you neutral. Being happy is a positive, active state. It is not a passive condition in which you accept happiness as though it were a gift. Creating the feeling of fulfillment, the euphoria that comes from achieving an important goal or overcoming a difficult obstacle requires your active participation.

There is a great deal of truth in the old adage that busy people are happy people. According to Fordyce, "Unhappy people waste a lot of time in idleness. Happy people keep busy and make sure they fit activities they enjoy into their daily schedule." The emotions are not always subject to reason, but they always respond to action. Completing a job we've been avoiding, exercising—just about any activity that makes us feel productive and useful—makes us happier people.

It is also true that happiness generally involves tradeoffs. Seldom can we do everything we wish; we simply don't have the time or stamina to fit everything into our lives that we would like. A career that demands long hours and working weekends requires cutting corners in the time spent with friends and family and less time in the pursuit of personal pleasures.

Use the following checklist to identify the things you want most from life, and what you realistically expect to achieve. Then determine what you must do differently to match your desires and expectations.

What Do I Really Expect From Life?

What do I want most from my career? _____

_____

_____

_____

What do I expect? _____

_____

_____

_____

What must I do differently to align my desires and expectations? _____

_____

_____

_____

What do I want most from my current job? _____

_____

_____

_____

What do I expect? _____

_____

_____

_____

What must I do differently to align my desires and expectations? _____

_____

_____

_____

What would I desire in an ideal relationship? _____

_____

_____

_____

What would I expect? _____

_____

_____

_____

What must I do differently to align my desires and expectations? _____

_____

_____

_____

What do I desire most from my current relationship?

_____

_____

_____

_____

What do I expect? _____

_____

_____

_____

What must I do differently to align my desires and
expectations? _____

_____

_____

_____

What do I desire most from my family? _____

_____

_____

_____

What do I expect? _____

_____

_____

_____

What must I do differently to align my desires and
expectations? _____

_____

_____

_____

What do I desire most from my social life? _____

_____

_____

_____

What do I expect? _____

_____

_____

_____

What must I do differently to align my desires and expectations? _____

_____

_____

_____

What else about my life would I like to change? _____

_____

_____

_____

What do I expect to do about it? _____

_____

_____

_____

What must I do differently to align my desires and expectations? _____

_____

_____

_____

You now have the beginnings of a blueprint for change. If you've answered all the questions honestly, you have taken the first step toward developing a realistic, achievable plan for your life. Future chapters contain the tools necessary to help you prioritize your objectives and set definite short-, medium-, and long-term goals to put your plan into action.

CHAPTER 4

RISK MINIMIZING

It was the stuff of an adventure novel. British billionaire Richard Branson and his copilot Swedish balloonist Per Lindstrand were the first human beings ever to cross the Atlantic Ocean in a hot air balloon. Their specially designed, oversize balloon had traveled 3,075 miles from Maine to the Irish Sea, a little farther than they had planned, but virtually without incident. It was a picture-perfect trip.

Then suddenly something went wrong. As they neared Ireland, they were quickly propelled upward by the winds and were blown out over the Irish Sea. As they evaluated their situation, it seemed that the best bet was to parachute out and hope for a quick rescue.

Lindstrand bailed out, leaving Branson, who had learned to fly the balloon only a couple of months before, in charge. In an interview in Virgin Airways' New York office, he recalled his feelings: "I wasn't really feeling too much in control," he said in characteristic British understatement. "Standing on top of the (specially designed pressurized) capsule, I wasn't even sure I had put on my parachute the right way. As I looked down at the clouds below . . . I had done two parachute jumps in my life, neither of which had been particularly successful. . . . It was very lonely; the fuel was almost gone, and I was desperately trying to decide: Should I jump or shouldn't I?"

In what he would later describe as "one of the most important decisions of my life," he decided that if he was going to live only for a few more minutes he would wait until the last of the fuel was used up. He climbed back into the capsule to clear his mind and give himself time to think. "I tried to decide if there was any alternative besides attempting to parachute into the sea at eight o'clock at night, which at the time didn't seem like a particularly good idea to me.

"My conclusion was that I would use the balloon as a parachute and not the parachute itself. I would ride the balloon down." The balloon continued its slow descent, and when it popped through the clouds, Branson was amazed to see that he was virtually surrounded by helicopters. In an example of what has become known by his friends and associates as the "Branson luck," he had flown straight into the middle of a military exercise. He scarcely got his feet wet before he was picked up by a rescue helicopter.

Richard Branson is the founder and "president for life" of Virgin Records, which numbers Phil Collins, Janet Jackson, The Rolling Stones, and Boy George among its artists, and the founder and chairman of Virgin Airways (which now gives the giant British Airways fits on some competitive routes). He has used his incredible luck, his impeccable sense of timing, his shrewd business sense, and his love of adventure to capture the public's fancy and build a number of successful businesses. In the process, he has become one of the most admired entrepreneurs in the world and was recently rated by British students as the third most admired man in the world.

Branson is a self-styled "adventure capitalist" who has water skied behind a blimp, parachuted from airplanes, and was delivered to his own wedding dangling from the landing struts of a helicopter. He has crossed the Atlantic twice in a speedboat and the Atlantic and the Pacific in a hot air balloon. He holds the world speed record for all three crossings. Branson is a man whose chief requirements are met, according to Fred Goodman's 1992 article in *Vanity Fair*, "whenever a great force of will can be set against singularly bad odds."

Yet, Branson does not see himself as a risk taker. "I don't like taking risks," he says. "I know that sounds contradictory to the balloon thing, but I think I'm protected against the downsides before going into something." When he began Virgin Airways, he recognized at the outset that the airline business was risky. To cover himself, he leased one airplane that his crews flew between London and New York, and he structured the lease with Boeing so that he could return the plane at the end of the first year if things didn't work out. His total financial risk going in was a one-year lease. All other costs were variable and controllable.

Things did work out. Today, Branson is chairman and CEO of a $1.3 billion travel and entertainment conglomerate, the third-largest privately owned company in Britain. Virgin Airways has several major expansions planned for the 1990s, including introducing service to new destinations in the United States and Africa and expanding service already provided to several cities. Plans also include expansion of Branson's hotel and other travel-related businesses.

Unlike popular folklore, Branson and other successful entrepreneurs are not risk takers. Neither are they risk averse. They are *risk minimizers*. They learn as much as they can about a prospective venture, study their options very carefully, and make a "go or no go" decision. They are not prone to "analysis paralysis," nor are they crapshooters who risk everything on a whim.

The key is that after they study the situation and evaluate the alternatives—they take action. They do something. They advance their businesses or go where no one has ever gone before because they are willing to try something that they have never done because they are confident that it will succeed. They have done their homework.

They also know that sometimes things don't work out, so, as Branson did with his first leased airplane, they cover the downside. They have, admittedly informally at times, established acceptable minimum levels of success and developed an exit strategy. They have a pretty good idea what they will do in any eventuality. If the business or the adventure doesn't work out, they don't view it as a massive failure and become despondent. They simply learn from the experience and try something else.

Risk minimizing means making a number of informed decisions. In any important, complex situation, success seldom follows a snap judgment or a single decision. When an opportunity presents itself, or you are jolted with a flash of inspiration, the first step in evaluating the possibilities is to learn as much as possible about the subject. Read periodicals and books, conduct database research, talk to friends, relatives, and people in the field. Above all, use your own good sense. If something seems too good to be true, it probably is.

It is also important to note in minimizing risk that accurate thinking is not an act; it is a process. Research is followed by careful analysis and evaluation of all possible alternatives. Successful people use various techniques, but they always try to prepare for any eventuality. Winston Churchill tried to anticipate every possible question before he made a speech about an important subject. He developed and rehearsed the answers before he made the speech. He minimized the risk of failure by careful preparation.

The next step in the risk minimizer model is to take action. At this point, it is important to limit the scope of the action and its corresponding consequences. Richard Branson did not buy a fleet of 747s because he thought Virgin Airways was a good idea. He leased one airplane and tried it out. Most companies, for example, wouldn't think of introducing a new product until they had tested the packaging, the advertising, the public perception of the name, and a host of other variables—in addition to the product itself—before launching it on a grand scale. It is simply too expensive to introduce a new venture in today's marketplace without testing it first.

Results from initial tests are then evaluated, research is analyzed, and options are reconsidered. Adjustments to the original idea are made as necessary; then, the product is tested again. This time it might be tried in a larger region or on an audience with a different demographic profile. The process is repeated until all the bugs have been worked out.

Only then are large advertising budgets planned, people hired, and commitments made.

As time passes, repetitive patterns are developed by the makers, sellers, and buyers of the product. Because things are working, habits are developed. We do things the same way because we no longer have to think about them. Habits are a shortcut to getting the job done more efficiently and more quickly so we can devote our energies to something more challenging. Unchecked, habits are also dangerous. They can lead to complacency.

After the product has reached a certain level of success, it becomes known and accepted by customers, and it experiences more or less regular increases in sales. Although McDonald's fast food is sold around the world today and the golden arches are a part of the American landscape, founder Ray Kroc started his company with one hamburger stand in Des Plaines, Illinois. He refined the making and selling of burgers until the process was perfected; only then did he begin selling franchises to others.

Just when things are going great, something else happens—competition. In the McDonald's case, it was Burger King; others quickly followed with a promise of a better burger because it was cooked differently, or better service, or some other competitive advantage. McDonald's, like every other company or individual with a new idea, had to innovate and improve to remain competitive. With each innovation or improvement, the risk-minimizing process starts over again.

Figure 1 shows a model of how the process works.

Although the process was developed for the business world, the techniques are adaptable to any portion of our lives. If we use it to make decisions about anything that is important to us, we significantly increase the likelihood of success and greatly minimize the chance of failure. Even if we do fail, our exposure is limited and the risk is managed. In addition, the information we gain from the experience will be valuable in the future. The net effect of the entire process is that we

Figure 1. Risk minimizer model.

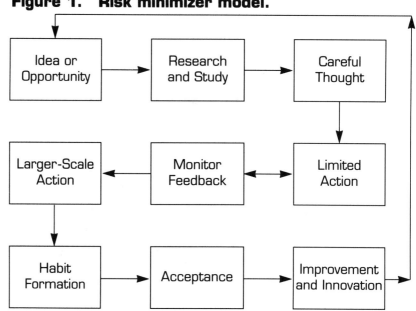

gain confidence and our self-esteem is improved. Because we succeed, we are more willing to take on new challenges.

Everyone has difficulty making decisions occasionally, according to psychiatrist Philip D. Cutter, medical director of the Mental Health Center of Greater Cape Ann, Massachusetts. According to a 1991 *Redbook* article by Sandie Horwitz, Dr. Cutter believes "It's difficult to know what to do in every situation—and it isn't sensible to make snap decisions on really important issues. But when indecisiveness begins to interfere with a person's daily functioning, then it becomes a problem. And often there are underlying causes for what's happening."

Lead, follow, or get out of the way!

—LEE IACOCCA

Experts say our aversion to risk is often directly linked to what we learned about decision making as young children. If our parents were decisive and encouraged us to take sensible risks and to learn new things, the chances are good that we will behave in that manner. We learn very early in life what our boundaries are and how to make decisions that have a positive effect.

It's tougher for us if our parents agonized over the most minute decisions and suffered endlessly over important ones. The subtle message we learned by observing them is that decisions are difficult and that any risk, however small, is something to be avoided. Children of such parents tend to react in one of two ways: They either follow the same pattern as adults, or they take great pains to ensure that they do the opposite.

Laura, a 42-year-old writer, didn't give much thought to her decision-making habits until she began researching an article on the subject. She had always been a decisive person; if anything, she made decisions too quickly. A quick study in most subjects, she could analyze the pros and cons of a situation, decide what to do, and get on with it. For as long as she can remember, she has been a decisive, action-oriented person.

She didn't agonize, even with major decisions, but seized career opportunities with gusto even if it meant moving across the country. She would decide to purchase a new automobile and choose the make, model, and color in a single afternoon. Leasing an apartment or buying a house might take longer, but never more than a few days.

Although her decisiveness usually worked well for her, Laura occasionally experienced problems because of it. The red sports car didn't prove very practical for long trips or vacations, and the low property taxes in her neighborhood couldn't support a good public school system. She realized that she was overcompensating for what she had learned as a child. Her father couldn't make up his mind about a career and drifted from job to job, whereas her mother vacillated on every decision from what to wear each day to deciding at what age her daughter should be allowed to date.

Since learning that she was overcompensating, Laura is doing better. She hasn't become indecisive, but she is more likely to study important decisions a little longer, making sure she has all the information necessary to make an informed choice.

Experts offer some tips that may be helpful in being decisive without making snap judgments:

- *Take your time with important decisions.* Seldom do they have to be made instantly. Sleep on it. You are more objective twenty-four hours later.
- *Recognize that life is not made up of true/false or multiple choice questions.* Usually there are several answers, any of which may be "right" or "wrong."
- *Remember that every decision has consequences.* Determining what they are will help you make an informed decision.
- *Make sure you put the decision in proper context.* All decisions are not equal. If the consequences are insignificant, the situation merits very little concern.
- *Be aware that no one else can make decisions for you.* Never let another decide important matters for you and don't blame them for a failed attempt when things go wrong. Your decisions are yours alone. Accept responsibility for them.
- *Keep in mind that seldom are decisions irrevocable.* If you make the wrong one, usually you can go back and fix it.

Depend not on another, but lean instead on thyself . . . True happiness is born of self-reliance.

—THE LAWS OF MANU

After you've made a decision, give it time to work. Don't give up or change your mind just because things do not immediately work out the way you expected. Most things take time, particularly when other people are involved. Because you are excited about a new idea or opportunity does not mean others will automatically follow suit. They may be envious or they may simply not care one way or the other. If it was a good decision yesterday, the chances are that it will still be solid today and tomorrow.

Remember, you've had time to think things through, you've done your homework. Give others the same opportunity. Usually, they will come around. But even if you have to go it alone, if you have made a careful, thoughtful, informed decision, you will have the courage of your convictions.

Knowing you are right will keep you strong when the going gets tough—and it almost always does.

Go the extra mile to make sure that you give your idea or opportunity a fair chance. Those who achieve great success in life are people who give more than is expected of them. They become indispensable to their bosses or their clients and customers because they can always be counted upon. They are there when they are needed, and they collect rewards commensurate with their efforts.

The foundation whose mission it is to perpetuate the teachings of master motivator Napoleon Hill developed a formula for it. It is:

$$Q + Q + MA = C$$

The **Q**uality of service rendered, plus the **Q**uantity of service rendered, plus the **M**ental **A**ttitude in which it is rendered, equals your **C**ompensation in the world and the amount of space you will occupy in the hearts of your fellow man.

Going the extra mile also provides additional benefits:

- It makes you more proficient at what you do.
- Others will respond in kind. Because you can be counted on to give more than expected, your boss, customers, or clients will give you better opportunities and more responsibility.
- You will like yourself better and so will your friends, family, and coworkers. It is hard to dislike one who always works harder, runs faster, jumps higher, and digs deeper than everyone else.
- Because you know how much more you have to do, you will be less inclined to procrastinate. You will become a person of action, one others recognize as an individual who "gets things done."

Perhaps the most helpful information in making decisions is the knowledge that all of life is a risk. The best we can hope for is to be sensible in our approach to decision making and prudent in the risks we choose to take. The key, nevertheless, is to take action. If we never attempt to do anything different, we most certainly will never expand our capabilities and begin to achieve at the highest levels of our capacity. Secretly, we all know we are capable of doing more, but we blame circumstances or other people for not allowing us to excel.

The choice is ours and ours alone. No other living person can makes us a success or failure. They can help, to be sure, but in the end what we do with our lives and careers is up to us. If we analyze the risks, make informed decisions, and take appropriate actions, the opportunities available to us are limitless.

Following is a list of a few people who made choices to do something different with their lives. You can, too, if you choose to do so.

Personality	Former Occupation
Sean Connery, actor	Truck driver and bricklayer
Gerald Ford, president	Male model
George Foreman, boxer	Electronics assembler
Boris Karloff, actor	Real estate salesman
Golda Meir, prime minister	Schoolteacher
Marilyn Monroe, actress	Factory worker
Elvis Presley, singer	Truck driver
Ronald Reagan, president	Actor
Henry David Thoreau, philosopher	Schoolmaster and pencil maker

CHAPTER 5

STEPPING-STONES OR STUMBLING BLOCKS

Every weekday afternoon at three o'clock, Paula Penny-packer goes on the air at WSPD-AM in Toledo, Ohio. Her show, a lively mix of conversations with politicians, callers, authors, and local and national thought leaders, is popular with listeners and advertisers alike. Pennypacker became a local celebrity, a talk show hostess, by losing an election.

In 1991 when no one from the Republican establishment wanted to tackle Toledo's formidable Democratic party machine, Pennypacker volunteered. "They laughed at first," she recalls, "but when I came within thirty-one votes of the mayor in the primary, they began to take me seriously. That's when they brought out the big guns." Thirty-three-year-old Pennypacker not only had to fight what she described as the rich and powerful Democrats who would "squash you like a bug," she also had to contend with the Republican "old boy network."

She expected problems, but not of the magnitude she experienced. One political expert told her that in political campaigns, disasters almost always come in threes. He proved to be prophetic. The first came when someone she trusted turned out to be a spy who gave copies of her plans to the opposition. The second occurred when the chairman of her own party took a European vacation during the critical final two weeks of the campaign, sending a message to voters that he did not support her. The final disaster? "Losing the election with 41 percent of the vote," she says.

Paula Pennypacker was born on May 3, 1958, the sixth of the seven children of Paul and Bette Pennypacker. She at-

51

> **Whatever women do, they must do it twice as well as men. Luckily, this is not difficult.**
>
> —CHARLOTTE WHITTON

tended parochial school and a Catholic high school, participated in Brownies, Girl Scouts, church league basketball, and the church youth group. She also struggled with the insecurities that most young people face in growing up.

THE FIRST LESSON

In a conversation at WSPD studios and in a telephone interview at a later date, Pennypacker talked about her life. "I was an ugly, skinny, flat-chested, freckled redhead," she recalls. "I didn't really develop until I was in college. Jane Fonda inspired me to start an exercise program and I developed myself." Pennypacker found that an unexpected side benefit of fitness was improved self-confidence. As she began to feel better physically, she began to think better of herself. Her newfound physical confidence expressed itself in more confidence about her overall appearance and her capabilities. No longer negative about her appearance, she began to believe that because she liked herself, others would also.

Pennypacker became so involved in her workout program that she used the skills she learned as a communications major at the University of Toledo to produce and market her own exercise video. Eventually, she quit her sales job to run her own video production company and promote her exercise videos. Along the way, she met and married Craig Spear, whose interests in video paralleled her own. However, the strains of the business, marriage, and Pennypacker's passion for politics proved to be too great. After four years, both the company and the marriage dissolved.

Encouraged by her mentor, a retired Marine Corps major general, grocery magnate, and Republican party leader, Walter A. Churchill, Pennypacker immersed herself in politics. It was a source of great pride that in her, thousands of others seemed to find a voice. She told reporters on primary election day that she would be happy if she received 10,000 votes. She got almost twice that many.

The Toledo *Blade* wrote: "For Republican Paula Penny-packer, the results of yesterday's mayoral primary election was a much needed jolt of adrenaline, a momentum builder for the remaining seven weeks of the campaign, and a clear message that she is a candidate to be taken seriously."

OPPORTUNITY IN ADVERSITY

The mayor prevailed in the general election, but Pennypacker carried a whopping 41 percent of the vote. Reminiscing about the election, she said, "I may have lost the battle and won the war. In politics—as in many things—success is a combination of luck and timing. It was because of the election that I was offered this position. I don't know if I will run for public office again or not, but I do know that I am going to keep my options open and do my best on the radio.

There are plenty of people who will ride in the limousine with you. What you want is someone who will take the bus with you when the limo breaks down.

—OPRAH WINFREY

"There really aren't very many good women commentators, so I have an opportunity to establish myself as one. Besides, I think I may be a better commentator than politician. My father told me that I'm too honest to be in politics. I don't like all the pandering—to labor unions, newspapers, and other influential people and organizations—one has to do in politics. Maybe, like a tree, I've been planted."

LESSONS FROM LOSING

What did Pennypacker learn from the experience? First, that defeat is never permanent unless you allow it to be. "People ask me how I deal with losing the election or with people taking shots at me on the radio program," she says. "I tell them it's water off a duck's back. When you are convinced you are right, you have to have the courage of your convictions. You have to believe in yourself and ignore the critics.

"Second," Pennypacker advises, "surround yourself with positive people and stay away from those who are negative.

Don't trust everyone who wants to be your friend. People are not always what they seem, and in politics in particular there are always plenty of people around who want to share in your successes, but they always seem to disappear when the going gets tough.

"Third, don't take things personally. Learn to separate your professional failures from your feelings about yourself as an individual. In politics, business, law, entertainment, or just about any other field, there are times when you succeed beyond your expectations, and there are times when you fail. The key is to learn from unsuccessful ventures. Don't make the same mistakes. Eventually, if you persist, you will succeed," Pennypacker advises.

GENDER DIFFERENCES IN SOCIETY

No one can make you feel inferior without your consent.

—ELEANOR ROOSEVELT

We live in an interesting time. Western society is struggling to discard the myth of an "ideal" family life in which the father works, the mother manages an immaculate household, and together they raise perfect children. The new American dream is likely to be closer to the reality of working parents, latchkey kids, blurring of male and female roles against a backdrop of the pervasive and difficult problems we face in contemporary society.

Women in particular must break out of stereotypical roles that have negatively impacted their self-esteem, and with women now accounting for about half of the work force (including increasing representation in management ranks), men must learn to be more sensitive to gender differences. Interestingly, for the most part males and females are not born with different opinions of self-worth. They are learned.

A recent study of more than 90,000 sixth-, ninth-, and twelfth-grade students conducted by the Minnesota Department of Education revealed some disturbing findings. Until they reach puberty, boys and girls have a pretty equal view of their abilities to deal with life's challenges. By the time they reach the ninth grade, however, Claire Berman, in

Ladies Home Journal, November 1990, reports that "the number of positive responses from girls had plummeted. According to the study, by that time "females were twice as likely as males to believe they don't have much to be proud of, can't do anything right and are no good."

In the article there is speculation that the decline in feelings of self-worth is attributable in part to the emphasis society places on appearance, a message that is reinforced by advertising messages that use sex appeal to sell their products. Young girls try to emulate the thin attractive models they see in magazines and on television and are depressed when they can never quite measure up. They feel as if they have failed, and their self-esteem suffers as a result.

There is hope, but the process of restoring diminished self-esteem can be a long and arduous one. In severe cases, therapy may be required, but for a great majority, workshops and self-help programs can be important contributors to a renewed sense of self-worth. It begins with how we react to our failures and deal with the disappointment of achieving less than we expected of ourselves.

A journey of a thousand leagues begins with a single step.

—LAO-TZU

It's been said again and again that the hardest part of any job is getting started. Almost nothing is as difficult as it first appears when we tackle it with enthusiasm and determination. Every time we try and fail, we become stronger, more capable people who will likely succeed next time.

Our strength grows as we struggle. Just as exercise strengthens muscles, overcoming obstacles teaches us to persist, to work harder and smarter, to eventually succeed. We become stronger, faster, and better at what we do. The strengths we gain through trying and failing make us stronger in every other aspect of our lives as well.

When we do eventually succeed—and we will if we stay with it long enough, we develop newer and better ways of doing things. The techniques we develop through trial and error and trial and success teach us physical and mental shortcuts.

(Text continues on page 59.)

CAN I BE DEPENDED UPON?

You and others need to know that when you encounter obstacles along the way, you can deal with them, overcome them, and persevere until you succeed. Use the following checklist to determine how dependable you are when it comes to dealing with adversity. Circle the letter indicating

1. When faced with a difficult problem, my first reaction is probably to:
   a. Give up, assuming it is too difficult for me to handle.
   b. Get someone to help me solve the problem.
   c. Try a different approach.
   d. Postpone action, hoping the problem will work itself out.

2. In time of crisis, those who know me best will likely assume that I will:
   a. Panic.
   b. Remain calm and reassure those around me.
   c. Take a leadership role; help myself and others.
   d. Be able to take care of myself.

3. If someone asks for my help at a time that is inconvenient for me, I am likely to:
   a. Drop what I am doing and help.
   b. Tell him or her that ordinarily I would be happy to help but that I am very busy right now.
   c. Postpone helping, but set a definite date to begin.
   d. Become angry with them because they are too insensitive to notice that I am busy.

4. In relationships, I am most often the one who compromises to avoid conflict:
   a. True.
   b. False
   c. It depends upon the situation.

5. When someone in my department at work needs help on an important project:
   a. They come to me first.
   b. They ask me only when no one else is available.
   c. They ask me if they perceive it to be within my area of expertise.
   d. They never ask me.

6. When a friend or relative needs advice, they know I will:
   a. Demand that they take the action I think is best.
   b. Equivocate.
   c. Offer several suggestions for them to consider.
   d. Advise them of what I think is the best course of action.

7. You are part of a team responsible for a major project. What will you do if others get credit for a job well done while your contribution goes unnoticed?
   a. Nothing. That's what I get paid for.
   b. Assume that I didn't do that much anyway.
   c. Demand recognition from other members of the team.
   d. Quietly make sure management is aware of my contribution.

8. You've promised your spouse that you will attend a special dinner with him or her to-

(continues)

night. On your way out the office door, an important client phones. You:

a. Take the call. Your spouse will understand if you're late.

b. Tell the client you will phone when you reach home.

c. Have your secretary take a message.

d. Tell the client you are on your way out but will call first thing tomorrow.

9. You discover that you and your close friend (who is better qualified than you) have applied for the same position. You react by:

a. Withdrawing from the competition.

b. Subtly trying to discredit him or her in your interview.

c. Intensifying your efforts; you must win at all costs.

d. Telling the search consultant about your friend's good qualities, then doing your best to sell yourself for the job.

10. When faced with a difficult decision, the course of action you will most likely take is:

a. Doing what's right regardless of the consequences.

b. Considering the effect of your actions upon others.

c. Taking the action you consider most appropriate under the circumstances.

d. Doing what's best for you.

Scoring

Add the numbers corresponding to the letters that you circled and total your score.

1. a-0, b-2, c-3, d-1	6. a-1, b-0, c-3, d-2
2. a-0, b-1, c-3, d-2	7. a-3, b-0, c-1, d-2
3. a-3, b-1, c-2, d-0	8. a-3, b-2, c-0, d-1
4. a-3, b-1, c-2	9. a-3, b-0, c-1, d-2
5. a-3, b-1, c-2, d-0	10. a-1, b-3, c-2, d-0

Evaluating Your Score

26–30 points: Careful, you may be overdoing it. The idea is for others to be able to reasonably depend on you, not that you subvert your needs and desires to those of others.

21–25 points: Great! You're a friend everyone would like to have. You're dependable but self assured, someone upon whom others can depend, but not a spineless wonder who lives only to serve others.

15–20 points: You'll never make it in the diplomatic corps. You worry too much about yourself without much regard for others. Take an objective look at yourself. Would *you* like to work with you?

Fewer than 15 points: Are you sure you understood the questions? Your answers indicate that you vacillate between arrogance and martyrdom. Neither will win you any friends.

Because we know how to do things better, we have more physical and mental energy to devote to more difficult tasks. Obstacles to success make life far more interesting. Without them, there would be no challenges; without challenges, life would become merely tedious.

There is more benefit in failure than there is in success, according to sales and marketing consultant David Driscoll. He suggests, in *Sales & Marketing Management*, April 1989, that after a failed attempt, ask yourself not "What have I lost?" Instead, ask "What have I gained?" He points out that in sales there are far more opportunities to fail than there are to succeed. Good salespeople know that they are going to be rejected most of the time. They simply count each rejection as a no that they have gotten out of the way as they move toward a yes.

"The more we fail, the more we succeed, if we stay out there trying," Driscoll says. "It is a game based on the law of averages and percentages. However, we make it personal and upset the percentages. From this day forward, ask 'Why did I fail?' Examine the answers carefully. Did you confirm doubts and become more discouraged and not want to try again? Or, did you realistically seek solutions, not excuses?"

By depersonalizing rejection, we can more objectively evaluate our failures and learn from our mistakes. Driscoll's sales analogy is a good example. Effective salespeople recognize that selling is a process, not an event. It begins with establishing contact wth a qualified prospect, one who would be a likely buyer of your product or service and one who has the authority to make the final decision.

The next step is to arrange an appointment to deliver your sales presentation, demonstrate your product, or whatever means is most desirable to showcase your wares. Next comes the sales presentation and, finally, asking for the order. At any point in the process, the prospect can terminate it; the result is a lost opportunity for the salesperson.

If salespeople keep a record of each of those activities, very soon they learn how many calls they must make to secure an appointment, how many appointments they must obtain to make a sale, and how many sales they must make to reach their quota or earn the desired income. Thus they know at the outset that in order to be successful, they must take the initiative to make the required number of calls. When they do, the sales will take care of themselves.

Keeping track of percentages also identifies opportunities for improvement. If a particular salesman is having trouble getting appointments but is very good at closing the sale, think of the possibilities if he improves his calling technique. Dramatic sales increases will automatically follow. It is a matter of learning from previous mistakes and using the law of averages to his advantage.

> **Results! Why, man, I have gotten a lot of results. I know several thousand things that won't work.**
>
> —THOMAS A. EDISON

Thomas Edison was one of America's greatest success stories. His inventive genius paved the way for the technological revolution and literally changed the landscape of America. Without the power of electricity, we would have none of the modern conveniences that we enjoy today; without electricity to power elevators, for instance, there would be no skyscrapers. The height of the tallest building would be limited to our ability to climb stairs.

Yet, Edison was also one of our most spectacular failures. Historians tell us that he tried more than 10,000 experiments in his attempt to develop the incandescent light. His greatest problem was that when electricity generated enough heat to make the filament glow, it soon burned itself up. Only when he found the right filament and removed the oxygen from the bulb was he able to perfect the forerunner of today's electric light.

Failure is important in another sense, according to David Driscoll. "(It) renews our humility and prevents us from taking ourselves too seriously. Life is an adventure to be approached with a sense of humor. Failure is just for the fun of it. Failure shapes our objectivity."

TIME TO START OVER

Cowboys in the Old West had a colorful expression for sticking with the job until it was done: "There never was a horse that couldn't be rode, and there never was a cowboy that couldn't be 'throwed.' " They knew that sometimes you win and sometimes you lose and that some things require more effort than others, but if you persist, you will eventually prevail.

Cowboys also knew that the best time to get back on the horse was immediately after you had been thrown. That's the best time to learn from your mistake—while the lesson is clear in your mind—and certainly the best time to overcome the fear of failing again. Use the following as a guide to learning from your mistakes:

How to Learn From Past Mistakes

1. Why did you fail to do what you expected? Was it because you were poorly prepared, lacked a certain skill, or had unrealistic expectations? Be as specific and objective as possible. _____

   _____

   _____

   _____

2. What did you learn from the experience that you can constructively apply in the future? _____

   _____

   _____

   _____

3. Did external factors over which you had little or no control affect the outcome? If so, what were they?

   _____

   _____

   _____

4. What could you have done differently to minimize the risk of failure? _____

   _____

   _____

   _____

5. What knowledge or skill do you need to ensure that you do not make the same mistake again? _____

   _____

   _____

   _____

Nothing in the world can take the place of persistence. Talent will not; nothing is more common than unsuccessful people with talent. Genius will not; unheralded genius is almost a proverb. Education will not; the world is full of educated derelicts. Persistence and determination alone are supreme.

—ANONYMOUS

6. How will you obtain that knowledge or skill? _____

_____

_____

_____

7. Who can you call upon to help you obtain the knowledge or skill you need to succeed? _____

_____

_____

_____

8. Who has an interest in your success and would be willing to help you? _____

_____

_____

_____

9. What action should you take to ensure success next time? _____

_____

_____

_____

10. Why should you continue to try until you succeed? What are the rewards for success compared to the penalties for failure? _____

_____

_____

_____

CHAPTER 6

YOU ARE WHAT YOU THINK

Whatever the mind can conceive and believe it can achieve— with a positive mental attitude.

—W. CLEMENT STONE AND NAPOLEON HILL

It is very likely that during your life you will become what you think about most. If you are consumed by negative, destructive thoughts, you will be a sad and unhappy person. If you eliminate such thoughts and focus on positive things, you will become a happy, productive person.

It is a natural tendency of the mind to transform your thoughts into their physical equivalent. That's its job. Your mind is the central computer that tells you when to eat, sleep, and perform countless functions necessary for your survival and well-being. It is essential, then, that you control the input of your human computer. Otherwise, it will behave exactly as its mechanical counterpart does: garbage in, garbage out.

Like most important aspects of your life, managing your thoughts and your expectations for your career, education, family, friendships, and health and fitness is not something decided upon and promptly dispensed with. It is a programming process that is time-consuming and often tedious and difficult. But it works.

Success in any endeavor begins with having a clear fix on what you would like to accomplish. Without an established destination, one direction is about as good as another. Goal setting puts you in charge of your life. You determine where you would like to be at any given time and you establish your own goals—short-, medium-, and long-term—to help you get there. Without fixed goals, you are likely to drift, driven by random external forces and events that have no real meaning or purpose for you.

In simplest terms, developing a plan for your life is similar to organizing a cross-country trip. Both require you to have a definite destination in mind if you are ever to have any hope of arriving there, and both inherently contain interim objectives that must be met if you expect to reach your ultimate destination on schedule. A good plan will also have sufficient flexibility to accommodate detours and delays, and it will allow time for a side trip or two to check out interesting possibilities that arise unexpectedly.

ELEMENTS OF A GOAL

Setting a goal helps you focus all your thoughts and energy on what you wish to achieve. It ensures that you do not fall into an activity trap (assuming you are accomplishing something merely because you are keeping busy), and it keeps you on course when the environment is altered or unexpected events occur along the way. Such things may temporarily delay or deflect you from your objective, but if you have your goal firmly fixed in your mind, nothing can deter you for long. Obstacles are merely temporary inconveniences to be overcome in order to correct your course.

These are the four elements of a goal:

1. A clear, concise written statement of what you wish to achieve.
2. A plan for achieving your goal.
3. A timetable for its achievement.
4. A commitment to achieve the goal regardless of the obstacles to be overcome.

Your Written Statement

If ye have faith as a grain of mustard seed . . . Nothing shall be impossible unto you.

—MATTHEW 17:20

It is important to write down your goal. Thoughts are often vague and imprecise; a written sentence requires you to choose correct words and to be specific. We learn in school at a very early age that when the teacher says something is important, we should write it down because we very likely will be tested on the topic. Throughout our lives and careers, the message is reinforced: Almost everything important should eventually be committed to writing.

Writing down a goal also helps internalize it. Learning experts say that using more than one sense (sight, hearing, touch, smell, taste) facilitates learning and helps memory. Our thinking is clarified and our recollection of precisely what we wish to achieve is greatly enhanced by writing it down, studying, and memorizing it.

Your written goal need not be long. In fact, the shorter it is, the better. Limit it to a sentence or two at most and make sure it is easily understood. A good rule is: If it won't fit on a 3 × 5 index card, it is too long. If you require that much verbiage, you are not sufficiently focused. Take time to think your goals through and condense them into understandable, action-oriented sentences. Do not obfuscate something this important.

Your Plan

If you have no plan for achieving your goal, it is not a goal, it is a fantasy. You need a precise plan with definite action steps broken down into specific things that you must accomplish in the short, medium, and long term.

Let's say, for example, that your goal is to become the top salesperson in your company. Your short-term objective would be to sell enough to put you at the top of the list this week. A medium-term objective would be to become the top salesperson each month. In the long term, the objective would involve being the best this year and repeating the process and improving upon it every year thereafter. All activities would be directed toward the actions necessary to reach each milestone.

Good salespeople keep records of the number of qualified prospects (people who have purchase authority and an interest in the product or service) they contact to request an appointment to make a sales presentation. They also track the actual number of appointments, presentations, and sales that result.

Over time, they develop averages that can used to project future sales. They learn that in order to achieve a desired sales level, they must make the required number of calls. If they simply make the calls, sales will follow. The averages will hold—and even improve as the salesperson's skills improve. Such knowledge greatly reduces stress and minimizes the uncertainty of selling. If salespeople simply pay attention to the basics and do the right things, they will earn the incomes they desire.

This technique works with anything that is measurable. If you wish to lose weight, for example, establish an overall goal of losing a certain number of pounds, establish a deadline for completion, and determine how much you must lose each week to meet your goal. Determine the short- and medium-term goals that you must achieve to reach your ultimate objective.

Your fixed plan with its concise written goals serves as a guidepost to help you decide how you will spend your time. Each activity will move you toward your goal or away from it. Eliminate unnecessary, time-consuming activities that get you nowhere and focus on those that generate the greatest success.

Your Timetable

As with other elements of goal setting, a timetable should be precise, specific, and cut into bite-size pieces. It should include the activity to be completed and the time it is to be finished. Reaching the successful conclusion of any project will depend upon how well you manage each portion of it in order to complete the entire project on time.

Your timetable should take into account others who will be involved in the effort. Regardless of how important the project is to you, it may not be a high priority for others. Make sure that you allow time for review, modification, or participation by everyone who might have a stake in the project or be affected by its outcome. Begin with the project completion date and work backward, building in time for each activity. It is also a good idea to include a small cushion to allow extra time for glitches that always seem to occur.

As an example, let's assume you have been assigned the task of researching the viability of a new product. You are to work with outside consultants and people within the company to determine the size of the potential market, conduct market tests, develop a financial pro forma, and deliver your recommendations to management. Your timetable for major milestones might look something like the one below.

NEW PRODUCT EVALUATION PRODUCTION SCHEDULE

May 1	Management presentation.
April 15	Begin rehearsing presentation. Make copies of written report. Complete audiovisual materials.
April 1	Begin production of audiovisual materials and written report.
March 15	Make revisions and corrections to report.
March 1	Circulate draft report for comments and corrections.
February 1	Begin writing draft report.
January 15	Review consultants' findings, market research data, and interview transcripts.
January 1	Receive materials from consultants and staff assigned to project.

To measure your progress, remember that almost everything is measurable. It may be difficult to establish exact dates and times for career moves and promotions because they may depend on various outside influences, but it is possible to establish milestones or decision points. If your goal is to become a manager within five years, for example, and it appears around the fourth year that the promotion is not likely, perhaps it is a good time to start networking and get out some resumes. The promotion may come only with a change of jobs or companies.

Use your timetable to measure your success. The system works whether you are a corporate type, an entrepreneur, a professional services provider, or a public servant. Essential milestones are points at which you modify your plan to respond to changing circumstances or you achieve what you had planned and set new goals.

To budget your time, remember that the reason some people accomplish more than others is that they plan better and use their time more effectively. We all have the same twenty-four hours in each day; how we use them greatly influences what we achieve. Establishing goals for the various aspects of your personal, professional, and social life helps you set priorities. With a finite amount of time available and infinite demands upon your time, budgeting your time is as important—if not more important—than budgeting your money.

"Free" time during evenings and weekends is an important part of your time budget. It may be frittered away watching TV, or it may be spent in more productive activities such as catching up on personal matters, running errands, playing golf with a client, taking a graduate course, or attending a career development seminar. Often, what we do with our free time dictates whether our lives and careers will be punctuated by smashing successes or forever mired in mediocrity.

Use the grid on the next page to establish a weekly budget for your twenty-four hours of each day:

WEEKLY TIME BUDGET

	Mon.	Tues.	Wed.	Thurs.	Fri.	Sat.	Sun.	Total
Work								
Family								
Friends								
Exercise								
Education								
Personal								
Sleep								
Total	24	24	24	24	24	24	24	168

There is a great deal of truth in the old saw that "time is money." The table on the next page illustrates the value of your time at various income levels. Calculations are based on a forty-hour workweek with fifty-two weeks in each year for a total of 260 workdays each year ($40 \times 52 = 2080$ work hours per year; $5 \times 52 = 260$ work days per year).

Your Commitment

The trouble with cows, an old farmer once observed, is that they don't stay milked. The same is true with keeping a commitment. It is not something that is done once and forgotten. Changing your life requires reaffirmation of your commitment until it becomes a habit.

Most of us start out with the best of intentions (often around January 1 of each year), planning the improvements we wish to make in our habits and our lives. Then, reality gradually sets in, and we remember why we do things the way we do. It is easier, it is pleasurable, or it is part of a lifestyle

The Value of Your Time

Yearly Salary	Value of an Hour	Cost of Wasting One Hour Each Day for a Year
$ 10,000	$ 4.81	$ 1,250.60
15,000	7.21	1,874.60
20,000	9.62	2,501.20
25,000	12.02	3,125.20
30,000	14.42	3,749.20
35,000	16.83	4,375.80
40,000	19.23	4,999.80
50,000	24.04	6,250.40
75,000	36.06	9,375.60
100,000	48.08	12,500.80
150,000	72.12	18,751.20
200,000	96.15	24,999.00
250,000	120.19	31,249.40

developed over a long period of time. Eliminating bad habits and replacing them with good ones require discipline and determination.

Make it a practice to reaffirm your goal every day until it becomes a part of you. For years, Curtis L. Carlson, founder and chairman of the multibillion-dollar Carlson Companies, wrote down his goal on a little piece of paper and carried it in his wallet. Each day, he would take the paper out of his wallet and reread it and renew his commitment to achieving his goal. "When I reached that goal—sometimes the paper was frayed and dog-eared—I set a new goal and carried it.

"I carried it with me so I would always know it was there. It became a part of me. And because it was written, it became crystallized in my mind. It helped clarify my thinking and made it easier to make decisions. When you have a fixed goal, you can quickly evaluate whether your decisions will be toward your objective or away from it."

Carlson believes that going public with your goal is also an important part of making a commitment. If you tell others

> **Obstacles are those frightening things you see when you take your eye off the target.**
>
> **—CURT CARLSON**

about your goals, you won't give up on them as easily, he says. He built his company and acquired a personal fortune by institutionalizing goal setting in the Carlson Companies. There is never any doubt about his sales goals each year because the number is posted in the lobby of the headquarters building in Minneapolis. The goal permeates the organization, and managers and employees know what they are expected to contribute to the achievement of the goal.

Carlson ignores economic fluctuations, recessions, and other factors that are beyond his control and focuses on his goals with a intensity bordering on obsession. "All we have to do," he tells his managers, "is keep our eye on the target. Obstacles are those frightening things you see when you take your eye off the target."

W. Clement Stone suggests repeating your goal aloud several times in the morning and again in the evening. Look in the mirror and speak loudly and enthusiastically. Your subconscious mind cannot distinguish between truth and fiction. It believes what you tell it. If you repeat something often enough, your mind will accept it as fact and help you transform your goal into physical reality.

Visualization also helps to reinforce your commitment. Imagine yourself getting in your new automobile, feeling the texture of the leather seats, enjoying the aroma that uniquely designates a new car, and starting it up. Picture yourself unlocking the front door of the dream house you have just purchased. Think of what you will say when you congratulate your son or daughter upon graduation from a prestigious university. Post a photo in a prominent place of the car or house you desire or the campus of the university to which you plan to send your children. Look at it every day and reaffirm your commitment to achieving your goal.

There are few things in life that you cannot have if you make up your mind to get them, develop a workable plan, take the necessary action steps, and follow through with determination and dedication.

Use the following worksheet as a guide to help you develop your plan. Be sure to identify the short- and medium-term goals that you must achieve in order to reach your ultimate goal.

Personal Achievement Plan

Career Goals:

My major career goal is _____

_____

_____

I expect to reach this goal by _____

Medium-term goals:

1. _____

    Completion date: _____

2. _____

    Completion date: _____

3. _____

    Completion date: _____

Short-term goals:

1. _____

    Completion date: _____

2. _____

    Completion date: _____

3. _____

    Completion date: _____

Educational Goals:

My major educational goal is _____

_____

_____

I expect to reach this goal by _____

Medium-term goals:

1. _____

   Completion date: _____

2. _____

   Completion date: _____

3. _____

   Completion date: _____

Short-term goals:

1. _____

   Completion date: _____

2. _____

   Completion date: _____

3. _____

   Completion date: _____

Family Goals:

My major goal for my family is _____

_____

_____

I expect to reach this goal by _____

Medium-term goals:

1. _____

   Completion date: _____

2. _____

   Completion date: _____

3. _____

   Completion date: _____

Short-term goals:

1. _____

   Completion date: _____

2. _____
   Completion date: _____
3. _____
   Completion date: _____

Friendship Goals:
My major goal for friendship is _____
_____

_____

I expect to reach this goal by _____

Medium-term goals:
1. _____
   Completion date: _____
2. _____
   Completion date: _____
3. _____
   Completion date: _____

Short-term goals:
1. _____
   Completion date: _____
2. _____
   Completion date: _____
3. _____
   Completion date: _____

Health and Fitness Goals:
My major goal for health and fitness is _____
_____

_____

I expect to reach this goal by _____

Medium-term goals:

1. _____

   Completion date: _____

2. _____

   Completion date: _____

3. _____

   Completion date: _____

Short-term goals:

1. _____

   Completion date: _____

2. _____

   Completion date: _____

3. _____

   Completion date: _____

It's never too late to start:

Grandma Moses was painting at age 100. Mother Theresa won the Nobel Peace Prize at 69. Bertrand Russell was a peace activist at 94. Pablo Picasso created drawings and engravings at 90. Albert Schweitzer headed up a hospital in Africa at 89. Michelangelo completed the architectural plans for the church of Santa Mario degli Angeli at 88. Corazon Aquino was elected president of the Philippines at 53 following the assassination of her husband. Pablo Casals was giving cello concerts at 88. Winston Churchill wrote *A History of the English-Speaking Peoples* at 82. Adolph Zukor was chairman of Paramount Pictures at 91. George Burns won an Oscar for his performance in *The Sunshine Boys* at 80.

CHAPTER 7

THE ART OF
BUILDING RELATIONSHIPS

No man is an island entire of itself; every man is part of the main.

—JOHN DONNE

Only the incredibly bright or the incredibly lucky—or both—can achieve lasting success alone in today's complex interdependent society. We learn by working with others, and we leverage our capability by forming relationships with those whose skills and attitudes complement our own. When the right combination of people works toward a common goal, the results can be awe-inspiring.

Andrew Carnegie, the great industrialist and philanthropist who founded the predecessor company of U.S. Steel, knew very little about the technical aspects of the steel business. His genius was in his ability to build a successful team. He is said to have coined the term "Master Mind Alliance" to define a group of his key executives who worked in perfect harmony to achieve their common goal.

Today, the term goes by different names—strategic intent, shared vision, strategic alliance—but the results are essentially the same. The idea is that when companies or individuals team up, they create a kind of intellectual and emotional synergy that builds upon itself and adds up to a force far more powerful than the contribution of each individual effort.

CONCEPTS TO LIVE BY

There is nothing magical about the process of building relationships. Each of us can enlist others to help us in the pursuit of our personal goals or we can get them to rally around our causes if we are willing to live by a few simple concepts discussed below.

You Deserve Friendship and Respect

The first rule of relationship building is that every one of us is worthy of the trust, respect, and friendship of others. Whatever opinion you may hold of yourself, wherever you are on the self-esteem scale, regardless of your doubts and insecurities, you are entitled to and should expect such things from others.

Have you ever met someone that you immediately disliked and regardless of how hard you tried you were unable to overcome your negative feelings about that person? There may be many reasons for such instantaneous instinctive reactions. It may be a wisp of a recollection locked in genetic memory; it may be that the person subconsciously reminded us of someone with whom we've had a bad experience; or it may simply be a first impression based on an insensitive comment.

Conversely, most of us have also had the opposite reaction. We have met people with whom we just seemed to click from the moment we were introduced. They were funny, witty, charming, intelligent—they possessed all the traits we like in a person. Sometimes we marry those people, sometimes we become business partners, and sometimes we later become bitter enemies.

The chances are good that the reason we respond so strongly to certain people is that we see in them the traits that we most like or dislike in ourselves. Or, we recognize behaviors that we desire and would like to emulate. We see them not for what they are; they become a dim reflection of ourselves as we are or would like to be.

The next time you have strong feelings—positive or negative—when you first meet someone, exercise caution. Such feelings may lead to problems or unrealistic expectations. Ask yourself: What is it about this person that I really like?

What specific behaviors or personality characteristics do I find attractive or unattractive? How is this person like me? How is he or she different? Am I really looking at a reflection of myself in this person?

Manage your emotions so that you feel entitled to his or her friendship instead of craving it because you are so favorably impressed or feeling guilty because you dislike the person and are not exactly sure why you feel the way you do.

People Are Fundamentally Good

The second concept of building successful relationships is that we must accept the idea that most people are inherently good. They may occasionally be rude, stubborn, irascible, and thoughtless, but they are fundamentally good. It is not something that can be proven scientifically, according to John-Roger McWilliams and Peter McWilliams, authors of *Life 101*, who say that for every psychologist, philosopher, and poet one could quote to prove that people are good, "those who believe that humans are fundamentally evil can quote just as many philosophers, psychologists, and poets—and their list of p, p, and p would probably outnumber ours."

The authors say that to prove goodness, all one has to do is go to the source of human life: Look into the eyes of an infant. "We've looked into the eyes of quite a few," they say, "and we have yet to see fundamental evil radiating from a baby's eyes. There seems to be a purity, a joy, a brightness, a splendor, a sparkle, a marvel, a happiness—you know: good." Children learn bad behavior the same way they learn good behavior—by observation and experience. The best rule of thumb is to assume people are decent until they prove otherwise.

It would be dangerously naive to assume there are no evil people in the world. There are far too many, but they *are* in the minority. We hear more about them because they get all the publicity. Good news doesn't sell newspapers or get high ratings on television.

In the business world, because selfish, ruthless, cruel people are also often ambitious, they frequently climb over others with abandon as they pursue their goals. They may even rise to high levels in the organization, but their tenure is usually brief. People who cannot inspire others to work with them never become leaders. Fear and intimidation work as a motivator for only a short time.

Others Like to Help You

The third concept of relationship building is that most people like to help others. It is another fact that cannot be scientifically proven, but if you doubt its veracity, try asking others for help or advice. Most people are reluctant to volunteer to help out because they don't wish to impose themselves where they are not wanted. The mere act of asking for assistance breaks down barriers.

Most of us also know—whether we admit it or not—that we have seldom achieved anything noteworthy without the help of others. We've all had spouses, lovers, parents, relatives, friends, coaches, teachers, and mentors who helped us grow and realize our potential. They encourage us to stretch, to try something new or more difficult because they believed in us. We learned that we were capable of more than we thought. Because we've received a hand from others, we are willing to lend a hand. Some people find helping others so personally rewarding that they make a career of it; they become teachers, ministers, and counselors.

Most people don't care how much you know until they know how much you care.

—JOHN MAXWELL

Trust Is Essential

The fourth concept of relationships is that they are all based on trust. A marriage or a love affair is doomed to failure when those involved do not trust each other, and all successful business relationships are built on a solid foundation of trust between the partners. Most business deals are agreed

A friend is a gift you give yourself.

—ROBERT LOUIS STEVENSON

upon first and the details worked out later in contracts, purchase orders, and other formal documents. As the saying goes, the best contract is the one that is put into a filing cabinet upon signing and never needed again.

Trusting others is not easy. We've all been disappointed at one time or another by someone we trusted, and such experiences tend to make us more cautious. The best argument for trusting others is that it is very freeing. If we accept others for what they appear to be until they prove otherwise, we no longer have to analyze their motives or speculate about their intent. Trust saves a great deal of time and emotional capital.

A Relationship Should Be a Good Deal

The fifth concept is that a relationship is not a good one unless it is good for everyone involved. It doesn't matter if it is an emotional commitment between two people or an alliance between nations; every participant must receive and perceive equal benefit from it. A one-sided alliance will not endure.

In building a relationship with others, it is a good idea to occasionally put yourself in the other party's shoes. Ask yourself: Would I be happy with this arrangement if our roles were reversed? Do I treat my partner(s) fairly? Does he or she get as much out of the relationship as I do? If the answer to any of these questions is no, you should rethink the agreement or adjust your behavior before the other person or organization does.

People who are building the successful businesses of the future are those who recognize the importance of relationships. Every company has relationships with its employees, its customers, its suppliers, and its stockholders. Each is fragile and must be nurtured if it is to endure. Disregard for the relationship will result in lost consumers, low morale, unhappy investors, and suppliers who take care of their other customers first.

Conversely, companies that work to build good relationships with all their publics will find that their customers, employees, suppliers, and investors remain loyal—even in difficult times—and that they recommend the company to their friends and associates. Smart executives know this and take advantage of it; they see a transaction as the first activity in an ongoing relationship.

HOW TO BUILD YOUR TEAM

Many people have an interest in your success. Your family, your friends, your business associates—even your banker—would like to see you succeed. These people and many others represent a reservoir of talent that you can tap. You probably already have in place a network of people with varied expertise who can become an integral part of your master mind or strategic alliance if you only organize it and take advantage of the opportunity.

Call upon them for advice and support, and give it in return. Consider it a great honor when someone asks for a favor, and if you can, do it quickly and to the best of your ability. There is always an implied *quid pro quo*. When you help someone else, they will do the same for you. Likewise, when you ask for help, be prepared to give help in return—cheerfully and enthusiastically.

Much of Bill Clinton's success in winning the 1992 presidential election resulted from the efforts of his extensive network of friends, advisors, business associates, and political allies that he had cultivated over the years. He corresponded with them, phoned them, sought advice, asked for assistance, and gave it in return for many years as he worked to establish himself. They rallied to his support when he needed them most.

You can also supplement the knowledge of your friends and associates with paid professional advice. Just as you should ensure that you have sound medical advice and care for your physical needs, you should engage an attorney, tax advisor, or other consultant whenever you need such specialized advice. Regardless of your financial condition, there are professionals whose services you can afford. Getting good advice before entering into a contractual arrangement or making a major financial commitment is not expensive. It is no advice or bad advice that is expensive.

Use the following worksheet to help you identify those people who can help you acquire the contracts, knowledge, and skills you need to achieve your goals. It is not necessary to like or know each of them. It is even possible to have a relationship with dead people—philosophers, authors, and statesmen, for example—because the most important aspect of a relationship is how we feel about others, not how they feel about us.

Your Team Roster

1. Name someone who is essential to you, the person who is your closest friend and supporter. It may be your spouse, a parent or other relative, your secretary or assistant, or your best friend. _____

   _____

2. Name a person who is highly competent and well respected in your field, someone whose work you could study and emulate. _____

   _____

3. Name someone you've heard of in a related field who might be helpful if you could get to know the person and/or his or her work. Example: a writer can benefit from a publisher, an editor, a graphic designer, a publicist. _____

   _____

4. Name a person who might serve as a mentor for you, helping to guide you in your business or profession, providing you with opportunities, or

teaching you the ropes. It may be a family friend or relative, someone within your company, someone you know in a professional society or trade group, or someone in a totally unrelated field. _____

_____

5. Choose three people (living or deceased) whom you admire, aspire to be like, and who might serve as a role model for you to emulate. _____

_____

6. Name a person (or persons) who can serve as a source of information and ideas in topics that interest you. The subject areas may include your business or profession, your hobbies, or anything else you think would be of value to you. _____

_____

7. Name your harshest critic. What might you learn from that individual that will make you better at your job or in your social or personal life? _____

_____

8. Name the most level-headed person you know, someone who always has his or her feet on the ground, someone who you may always call upon for good advice. _____

_____

9. Name someone in your company or industry who always seems to be in the know about opportunities for recognition and promotions. It may be a peer, a department head, a competitor, an executive search consultant. _____

_____

10. Name a good friend or close acquaintance with whom you can share your dreams and aspirations openly, someone who is trustworthy and likes you

for what you are, not for what you can do for
them. _____

_____

11. List the professional members of your team: your
doctor, lawyer, banker, investment counselor, tax
accountant, search consultant or employment
agency, and others who have a financial interest in
your success. _____

_____

Review the list of people who are members of your team—
even if they don't know it—and plan how you can better use
your team to achieve your goals. Use the chart below to list
the type of assistance you would like from each. Indicate
whether the responsibility is theirs or yours, the action to be
taken or the information you would like to obtain, what you
expect to happen as a result of this activity, and when you
expect to complete it.

TEAM RESPONSIBILITY CHART

Team Member	Responsibility	Action to Be Taken or Info Needed	Expected Result	Due Date
1				
2				
3				
4				
5				
6				
7				
8				
9				
10				
11				

CONTAGIOUS ENTHUSIASM

One of the surest ways to get others on your side is to approach every task with enthusiasm. Even if you don't feel particularly enthusiastic, if you force yourself to act enthu-siastically, soon you will feel the genuine emotion. Acting decisively and enthusiastically is the first step toward *becoming* decisive and enthusiastic.

The best way to generate enthusiasm is to do something you really like doing. If you hate your job, it will be very difficult to be enthusiastic about it. (If you do, you should think about doing something else or examine your attitude toward your job and those you work with.) Conversely, it is virtu-ally impossible to do something you like without being enthusiastic about it.

Long before the cosmetics company she founded became known all across America, Mary Kay Ash discovered when she was a young housewife and mother that she could sell by the sheer force of her enthusiasm. Fascinated by a set of books that she desperately wanted because she thought they held the answers to virtually every problem mothers face with their children, she almost cried when she found out how much they cost. The saleswoman, sensing her interest and hoping for a sale, left the books with Ash over the weekend.

When the saleswoman returned for the books, Ash told her that she was going to save until she could afford them because they were the best she had ever seen. "When she saw how excited I was," Ash recalled later, "she said, 'I'll tell you what, Mary Kay, if you sell ten sets of books for me, I'll give you a set.' "

Ash thought this was a wonderful arrangement. She called her friends, neighbors, the parents of the kids in her Sunday School class. "I didn't even have the books to show them," she said. "All I had was my enthusiasm." She sold the ten sets of books in a day and a half and so strongly believes in enthusiasm that she made "I've Got That Mary Kay Enthusiasm" (to the tune of a popular hymn) a part of the culture at Mary Kay Cosmetics.

Enthusiasm sells. You can prove it to yourself by trying the following experiment.

Demonstrate Your Enthusiasm!

In the space below, write down one of the things that you enjoy in life, perhaps the thing you enjoy talking about more than anything else. _____

_____

_____

_____

_____

At the earliest opportunity, make it a point to bring up this subject when talking to someone. Pay particular attention to how you discuss the subject. Speak softly, avoid eye contact, and do not use hand gestures. How did the person with whom you talked react? _____

_____

_____

_____

How did you feel? _____

_____

_____

_____

Repeat the experiment with a different person, but this time speak up, maintain eye contact, use gestures, and move around. Note the difference in how your conversation partner reacted this time. _____

_____

_____

_____

How did you feel? _____

_____

_____

_____

You will begin to see the difference when you use the power of enthusiasm. It is worth noting that the definition of the word itself comes from the Greek words *en* (within) and *Theos* (God). Roughly translated, enthusiasm means "God within." Enthusiasm is not something you catch from someone else; it is something you generate within yourself.

EFFECTIVE LISTENING

The last word on the subject of relationships regards the importance of listening. Every good salesperson knows that listening is often far more critical in making sales than is talking. By listening to prospects, the salesperson learns about his or her prospective buyer's hopes and dreams, problems, and needs. He or she can then tailor the sales presentation to focus precisely on how the product or service can help. We are far more interested in the benefits to us than the features of the product or service.

Use the following quiz to determine your listening power.

Are You A Good Listener?

Score yourself on these personality traits to determine how effectively you listen. Use a scale of 1–10 with 10 being outstanding and 1 being poor.

Rating: *Attributes:*

_____ 1.   I usually find other people genuinely interesting.

_____ 2.   I am curious about what makes people tick and enjoy learning more about them.

_____ 3.   I think listening is generally easy and comes naturally to me.

_____ 4.   I empathize with the speaker.

_____ 5.   I am not distracted by things going on around me when I am listening to someone.

_____ 6.   I attempt to minimize distractions and interruptions when the environment is within my control (in my home or office, for example).

_____ 7.   I make it a point to maintain my composure and never let my emotions run away with me when I am listening to another person.

_____ 8.   I ask friendly questions to encourage others to talk more.

_____ 9.   I am not embarrassed or intimidated when I don't fully understand something; I simply ask them to explain.

_____ 10.   I try to focus on the central point of the conversation.

_____ 11.   I restate important points to make sure I understand key issues.

_____ 12.   I try to create a nonthreatening environment to encourage open discussion.

_____ 13.   I smile and nod when others speak to let them know I am interested in what they have to say.

_____ 14.   I force myself to focus on what the other person is saying even if I don't find it particularly interesting.

_____ 15.   I do not let my mind wander or think about what I will say next when someone is talking to me.

_____ 16.   I maintain eye contact in a conversation.

_____ 17.   I am very conscious of my body language and make sure I am in an open and accepting position when I listen.

_____ 18.   I observe the other person's body language and consider it an important part of the communication process.

_____ 19. I do not try to anticipate what someone will say next and complete their sentences for them.

_____ 20. I do not interrupt when others are speaking.

_____ 21. I never say "let me finish," or make similar statements when someone interrupts me.

_____ 22. I do not raise my voice to drown out or overpower my companion's comments.

_____ 23. I am not judgmental about others.

_____ 24. I don't make up my mind about a subject until I've heard all the facts.

_____ 25. I always try to be the kind of listener I would like to have as a listener.

_____   Total Score

Scoring

Add up the total of all your scores and rate yourself as follows:

225–250   You are a saint. Canonization will probably occur during your lifetime.

200–224   Start shopping for a new wardrobe. You will soon be everyone's favorite dinner guest.

175–199   You are a pretty good listener, one with whom your friends and associates enjoy conversing.

150–174   You are a better than average listener, but your attention drifts. Work on it.

125–149   You are about average. You think about what you are saying or plan to say about as much as you listen.

100–124   You are catching less than half of what is being said. Are you napping? Have a cup of coffee and get back in the game.

99 and
below   Either you are a very harsh critic of yourself or it's time for serious action. Use the questions on this quiz as a guide to help you strengthen your listening skills.

> **The most difficult secret for a man to keep is his own opinion of himself.**
>
> —MARCEL PAGNOL

CHAPTER 8

YOUR BELIEF SYSTEM

Life, an old fisherman once observed, is a lot like trout fishing. When you wade into the stream to cast out for whatever may await you, unless you have your feet firmly planted, you will just move with the current. You will drift, unable to withstand the forces that push you in whatever direction they happen to be going.

To avoid aimless drifting, you must have grounding philosophy, a belief system that you have carefully and thoughtfully developed for yourself. Otherwise, you must invent a new one every time you face a major decision in your life. Having a strong belief system helps you choose between difficult alternatives and keeps you on a firm footing as the currents of life swirl about you.

A SUCCESS PHILOSOPHY

One person who saw the need to formulate her guiding philosophy was Paula Blanchard. From all outward appearances, Blanchard was on top of the world. She was married to her college sweetheart, an ambitious young lawyer who early in his career was elected to the U.S. Congress and went on to become governor of Michigan. They were ubiquitous in Michigan's social and political life; they had a delightful son and all the perks that accompany important government positions. As Michigan's first lady, Blanchard was a popular spokesperson for the state and worked full time as an unpaid special advisor to the Michigan Department of Commerce.

But something was missing. "I discovered that my life was horribly out of balance because so much of my time was devoted to my husband's work and his ambitions," Blanchard recalls. "There was very little time left for nurturing the marriage, for family, for leisure pursuits, and for spiritual things. There was no time left for all the other things that are important in my life: family, friends, leisure and recreation activities, time for private reflection, meditation, and prayer."

In an interview in her Southfield, Michigan, office, Blanchard reflected on her life: "I realized that I was moving into my forties and my life was out of control. I was leading someone else's life and not my own. Too often, when women think about what they want from life, they let other people's goals override their own. They do what their husbands or their bosses or their parents or their kids think they should do."

If I had my life to live again, I'd make the same mistakes, only sooner.

—TALLULAH BANKHEAD

That realization led Blanchard to a long period of introspection as she considered her options and attempted to come to terms with who she was as a person, what she expected from her life, and what she wanted from her marriage. "It forced me to sit back and look at my values because I had to decide what was most important to me and how I can lead a life that conforms to those values," she says.

The personal philosophy that emerged from Blanchard's experience guided the agonizing decisions she would make in the weeks and months that followed, and it is the belief system that sustains her today. During the months that followed the period of introspection, she filed for a divorce, moved out of the governor's residence in Lansing, completed course work on a master's degree in video production from Michigan State University, started her own audio/video production company, and changed her life.

Prior to her recent appointment as vice president of communications for the National Fund for the United States Botanic Garden, Blanchard was a vice president of Casey Communications Management, Inc., a leading midwestern public relations and public affairs counseling firm affiliated with Shandwick, plc. She was awarded the Distinguished Alumnae Award by the College of Education at Michigan State, holds honorary doctorate degrees from three universities, writes a monthly column for *Detroit Metropolitan*

Woman magazine, and is a frequent speaker on women's issues and other topics.

Set Goals

Like most other achievers, Paula Blanchard is a proponent of goal setting. She points to the method used by Bo Schembechler, the flamboyant, outspoken—and highly successful—former head coach of the University of Michigan football team and later general manager of the Detroit Tigers. "When he was coaching at U of M, Bo worked with the team to develop its goals and required every player to develop his own personal goals.

"He had each player write on one side of a card his goals as a player and on the other side, he wrote down the team's goals. Players were then required to carry the card in their wallets and read their goals at least once every day. Players never knew when Bo would ask them to recite their personal goals or the team's goals so they had to have them at the tip of the tongue. They had to learn them, memorize them, and read them every day."

Manage Risk

Setting goals, however, is risky because it involves choices and changes. "If you choose alternative A over B, you risk the loss of B. That is sometimes very frightening and paralyzes people," Blanchard says. She believes that managing risk is especially difficult for women.

"In spoken and unspoken ways, society expects women to be responsible for the security of their families. Women have been charged with tending the home, the place where the family comes to feel safe and secure. It has been a woman's responsibility to provide that environment. Change involves risk, and risk is the antithesis of security."

Select Role Models

Blanchard also believes that role models are important in the development of a personal success philosophy. "My mater-

> Self-help is the capacity to stand on one's legs without anybody's help. This does not mean indifference to or rejection of outside help, but it does mean the capacity to be at peace with oneself, to preserve one's self-respect, when outside help is not forthcoming or is refused.
>
> —MAHATMA GANDHI

nal grandmother has a great deal of influence on me and was the primary role model in my life," she recalls. "She was widowed at twenty-nine in the mid-1930s when her husband died of tuberculosis that he contracted in WWI.

"She was left at home with three children all under six years of age. To support them, she got a job teaching school in my home town of Clarkston, Michigan. In those days, she didn't need a college degree to teach. She taught for many years, never remarried, and raised three children by herself. Eventually she was required to go to college to get a degree and a teaching certificate, and she graduated from Eastern Michigan University in the same year my father graduated from that university.

"She took me to New York City on the train when I was eleven. She took me skating on the ice rink at Rockefeller Center, to Saks Fifth Avenue, and to Radio City Music Hall to see the Rockettes. She was in her fifties at the time. That was just the kind of thing she did. I only realized recently how remarkable she was for the time in which she lived. She wore the latest fashions, traveled all over the world, and had countless friends to whom she was always writing letters and getting mail from in return. She led a very full exciting life and taught me that it is possible to live a rich life by oneself."

Choose Mentors

Blanchard suggests taking an active role in seeking mentors. Read biographies or autobiographies to learn how successful people dealt with opportunities or faced challenges. Don't wait for those you admire to invite you to work with them and learn from them. Go to them, tell them you respect them, and ask them to be your mentor.

"Most people are flattered when you tell them that you like the way they operate or that you respect what they've accomplished in their career," Blanchard says. Identify both men and women mentors and invite them to lunch once a month. It's been very enlightening and helped me in my professional development. You can't sit around and wait to

It is more important to live the life one wishes to live, and to go down with it if necessary, quite contentedly, than to live more profitably but less happily.

—MARJORIE KINNAN RAWLINGS

The art of becoming wise is the art of knowing what to overlook.

—WILLIAM JAMES

be asked. It goes with taking control of your life, taking charge, taking responsibility for your own professional development and your own happiness.

"Nobody else will do it for you. You have to do it for yourself. If I had one message for a happy and productive life," Blanchard concludes, "it would be this: Life is an adventure and very little is impossible."

Establish Your Code of Conduct

As Paula Blanchard discovered, her philosophy of life had to come from within herself. Yours must come from within yourself. We are all different, with different educational and social backgrounds, personal experiences, religious training, and moral values. Your belief system must fit into the context of who you are and who you wish to become.

Perhaps the best of all codes of moral behavior can be summed up in one sentence: Do unto others as you would have them do unto you. If the Golden Rule were universally followed, it would ensure that every individual is treated with courtesy and respect and that we are all encouraged to achieve the highest level of success of which we are capable. Following the Golden Rule also creates an energy that attracts others who have similar beliefs. It is an extremely positive force.

Regardless of how others treat you, the Golden Rule is a good starting point for the development of any personal philosophy. If you make it a practice not to do anything to harm others—and to help them whenever it is reasonable and practical to do so—it benefits you more than others. When you are a kind, considerate, compassionate person, you like yourself better and you become more confident. Your self-esteem is elevated.

As you develop your code of personal behavior, it is important to clearly understand your standard of personal conduct—the level below which you will not allow yourself to go. Most religious faiths include instructions for individual behavior, as do laws, moral codes, ethics rules, and company policies. They may agree on some practices and diverge or say nothing in others, but general codes of conduct usually represent the *lowest* acceptable standard. To feel really good about yourself, you should strive toward a precept much higher than the lowest acceptable code of behavior.

Developing a belief system, a personal philosophy by which you live, is a great help in times of stress or when there are important decisions to be made. You don't have to stop and think about what is legal or ethical or moral. You instinctively *know* the correct course of action.

Gain Understanding

In his book, *Being Better Than You've Ever Been,* Dr. Frank Fleming relates a conversation with Japanese author Fukujiro Sono about *kan*, the Japanese quality of constantly striving to make the "correct" decision, one that is fair to all involved, not one that is based primarily on the selfish interests of the individual. It is a mixture of Eastern philosophy and management style that has played an important role in moving Japanese industry from imitation to innovation to the position of world leadership it enjoys today.

Making the correct decision, Sono believes, depends on being well informed and having the necessary data, "but there is more to decision making. In Japanese there are three ideograms that are pronounced *kan*. One has the meaning of feeling and sensitivity. Another has the meaning of intuition as gained from experience. The third means perception, looking at things in such a way that one looks into their true nature. I believe that for a decision maker, it is especially important to cultivate this last *kan*, the *kan* of insight. . . . Without making the effort to develop the three *kans*, a fine-tuned intuition born of experience and perception to see reality and discern the essence of things, no new creation will emerge."

The best method for developing the all-important *kan* of insight, Sono believes, is to work earnestly to achieve your goals—to believe in what you are doing—and to study constantly. He recommends reading books on history, philosophy, and religion to broaden your understanding and insight.

As you work to achieve your business and professional goals, make sure you spend a little time each day in the study of issues that are larger than yourself, your job, and your small circle of friends and family. Ponder the thoughts and ideas that will strengthen the foundation of your belief system, the things that will enable you to grow into a wiser, more insightful person.

Get Organized

There are few things that will not benefit from organization, and nothing bolsters self-confidence like the knowledge that you understand the job that needs to be done and have it organized in a sensible, logical fashion. Just as our universe runs on order and not chaos, so should we human beings.

Some people are list makers, others use daily planners, pocket calendars, personal computers, or one of many commercially available systems designed to help you get your life organized. There are numerous tools available to you; all you need to furnish are the desire and the discipline.

Make it a practice to stop and think about the task at hand before you jump in and begin flailing away at it. If you take the time to think about a job at the beginning, you will complete it far more efficiently than if you try one thing and then another until you eventually find something that works. Organization is a great time saver and allows you to focus on larger issues rather than struggling to complete routine tasks.

If you make personal organization a critical component of your success philosophy, you will earn the respect of everyone around you. Because you are organized, you will be more confident, and both attributes will enable you to achieve more. Being organized also relieves stress. If you write down your goals and have a plan for achieving them, you don't have to keep worrying about them and fearing that you might forget something. Best of all, you will gain heightened respect for yourself; you know that your life is under control—your control.

Maintain Personal Discipline

The engine that drives organization is personal discipline. It is the willpower, the determination, the strength of character that compels you to stay with the job until it is finished. Most important, it is the personality trait that sustains you when you take charge of your life. If you are a disciplined person, you know you can react positively to the most negative situation—you can handle whatever comes your way.

> I have to live with myself and so, I want to be fit for myself to know, I want to be able as days go by, always to look myself straight in the eye. I don't want to stand with the setting sun, and hate myself for the things I've done.
>
> —EDGAR GUEST

There is no easy way to develop personal discipline. It is the result of forcing yourself to do the right thing, to take the initiative to accomplish something when you'd much rather be doing something else. Personal discipline is developed one act and one day at a time until it becomes a habit to listen to your inner voice when it tells you to get going and take positive action instead of procrastinating and putting off until tomorrow what you should be doing today.

Developing personal discipline is made more difficult because discipline does not usually provide instant gratification. In fact, the first feedback you receive may be negative as others try to persuade you to forget about work and do something that is more fun. Nevertheless, if you stick with it, the rewards of personal discipline do eventually come. Those who can discipline themselves to perform difficult tasks, to do what needs to be done regardless of what others may say, are the people who earn the respect and big promotions that go with outstanding achievement. They become the leaders.

Personal discipline allows you to ignore the criticism of others and to stop blaming your heritage, your environment, bad luck, or other people for your situation. It allows you to recognize that you have had problems (like everyone else), but that you can and will overcome them. In all the world, you are the only person who is ultimately responsible for your successes, your failures, and your happiness.

Aim Higher

If there is one common characteristic of successful people, it is that they know where they are going. If you have no idea where you are headed, one direction is about as good as another. But all roads do not lead to the same place. Without specific goals and definite plans for how you plan to achieve them, it is unlikely that you will ever go anywhere worthwhile; certainly you will never realize your potential.

Make sure your personal philosophy includes goal setting. As discussed in Chapter 6, you need goals for your career, your family and friends, your education, your health and fitness—for every aspect of your life. Without goals, it is impossible to measure your progress because you do not know where you should be at any given point of your development.

Strive for Balance

As Paula Blanchard discovered, if you allow your life to get too far out of balance, decisive—and sometimes radical—action will be required to correct it. Life is sometimes like a pendulum. As we move from one extreme to another, we pass briefly through the center—the point of perfect balance—but we do not remain there for long. If we do not strive for balance, it is very likely that we will never achieve it until we are too exhausted to continue lurching between extremes.

As your philosophy of life evolves, make sure you consider the concept of balance. Decide for yourself how much of your time, energy, and emotion should be invested in your career, your relationships, your family, and your friends. Allow time for renewal, a time when you can do the things you like, the things that relax you and recharge your batteries.

Whether you are a religious person who believes that after death your spirit ascends to a far better place, a person who thinks this is pretty much it, or someone who believes the truth lies somewhere in between, most agree on one fact:

> I shall pass through this world but once; any good things, therefore, that I can do, or any kindness that I can show to any human being or dumb animal, let me do it now. Let me not deter it or neglect it, for I shall not pass this way again.
>
> —JOHN GALSWORTHY

Your trip through the physical plane will be exactly what you choose to make it. You can be happy and successful, or you can be a miserable failure. The choice is yours and yours alone.

WORDS TO LIVE BY

Over time, most goal-oriented people develop affirmations and self-motivators that they memorize and recall when they need a little encouragement to keep going. They may be favorite quotations, catch phrases, or slogans that stick in your mind because they have a crisp, meaningful message. Many have been provided throughout this book.

Choose those that you find most appropriate and helpful to you. Say them aloud several times each day until they become a part of you. Go to a private place (so others won't think you've gone completely off your rocker), look at yourself in the mirror, and repeat—with all the conviction and enthusiasm you can muster—one affirmation or one self-motivator twenty times each morning and twenty times each evening for a week. It should then be firmly ingrained in your memory and can be recalled whenever you need it.

Here are ten suggestions to get you started:

1. Don't procrastinate; do it now!
2. When the going gets tough, the tough get going.
3. I am a good person.
4. I deserve to be happy and successful.
5. I can have anything I want if I am willing to work hard enough and smart enough to get it.
6. He who hesitates is lost.
7. I *am* somebody!
8. I am what I think about most.
9. I am unique—a one-of-a-kind masterpiece.
10. All things are possible if you believe they are.

A SENSE OF SELF-WORTH

In the most basic sense, self-esteem is nothing more than the ability to like yourself. On the surface, it would appear that recognizing one has poor self-esteem and taking corrective action would be a simple matter. Of course, it is not. Your self-image has been developed over a lifetime of experiences—negative and positive—and you are the product of those experiences. One isolated event or decision will not eliminate the cumulative effect of those experiences.

It is possible, however, to change. You have seen positive changes in the lives of others, and you may have experienced them in your own life. If you have, you know that any positive change usually involes a great deal of time and persistence. This book has provided you with the tools to change the things you dislike about yourself and to more effectively deal with situations over which you have little or no control. You have everything you need; the rest is up to you.

You are capable of more than you think. You simply haven't tested yourself sufficiently to discover the greatness that is within you. Very few of us ever reach our highest possible level of achievement because we are willing to settle for less. We compromise because we are unwilling to pay the price of success.

We look around us and see that the majority of others are more or less in the same condition. We realize that success is not the norm; it is extremely rare. We take solace in the fact that we are not alone in performing at a level far below our capability. We convince ourselves that we are content to be "average" because of the vast numbers of others that we see in the great sea of mediocrity.

Do not succumb to this temptation. Fight complacency and conformity with every ounce of your strength. Self-esteem (and the success it brings) does not come from others nor is it a natural by-product of the environment. It is a rare commodity that can come only from within. Only when you look inside yourself can you find the power to keep you on a positive course. You *are* better than you think.

You have the power of self-esteem. You can successfully meet the great challenges that await you if you only unleash that power.

BIBLIOGRAPHY

Berkman, Harold W., and Christopher C. Gilson. *Consumer Behavior.* Encino, Calif.: Dickenson, 1978, p. 228.

Berman, Claire. "How to Make Yourself a Stronger Person." *Ladies Home Journal* (November 1990), pp. 99, 101.

Clements, Chase. "Pennypacker, McHugh Near Tie." Toledo *Blade* (September 11, 1991), p. 1.

Cypert, Samuel A. *Believe and Achieve.* New York: Avon, 1991, p. 25.

Driscoll, David. "The Benefits of Failure." *Sales & Marketing Management* (April 1989), pp. 47, 50.

Dyer, Wayne. "Great New Book—Happiness: You'll See It When You Believe It!" *Redbook* (July 1989), p. 120.

Fleming, Dr. Frank. *Being Better Than You've Ever Been.* Englewood Cliffs, N.J.: Prentice Hall, 1983, p. 107.

Goodman, Fred. "The Virgin King." *Vanity Fair* (May 1992), p. 172.

Hill, Napoleon. *PMA Science of Success Philosophy.* Columbia, S.C.: Napoleon Hill Foundation, 1961, 1983.

Horwitz, Sandie. "Decision, Decisions." *Redbook* (July 1991), pp. 42–43.

Jacoby, Susan. "Self-Esteem: You Can Have It (Almost) All the Time." *Cosmopolitan* (August 1991), p. 153.

McWilliams, John-Roger, and Peter McWilliams. *Life 101.* Los Angeles: Prelude Press, 1991, p. 61.

Scheele, Adele. "Career Strategies: Pigeonholed. How to Break Out." *Working Woman* (October 1991), p. 46.

Ullyott, Kathy. "The Pursuit of Happiness: How to Put More Joy in Your Life." *Chatelaine* (December 1990), p. 18.